ACTION FIGURE!

Doonesbury Books by G.B. Trudeau

Still a Few Bugs in the System
The President Is a Lot Smarter Than You Think
But This War Had Such Promise
Call Me When You Find America
Guilty, Guilty, Guilty!
"What Do We Have for the Witnesses, Johnnie?"
Dare to Be Great, Ms. Caucus
Wouldn't a Gremlin Have Been More Sensible?
"Speaking of Inalienable Rights, Amy…"
You're Never Too Old for Nuts and Berries
An Especially Tricky People
As the Kid Goes for Broke
Stalking the Perfect Tan
"Any Grooming Hints for Your Fans, Rollie?"
But the Pension Fund Was Just Sitting There
We're Not Out of the Woods Yet
A Tad Overweight, But Violet Eyes to Die For
And That's My Final Offer!
He's Never Heard of You, Either
In Search of Reagan's Brain
Ask for May, Settle for June
Unfortunately, She Was Also Wired for Sound
The Wreck of the "Rusty Nail"
You Give Great Meeting, Sid
Doonesbury: A Musical Comedy
Check Your Egos at the Door
That's Doctor Sinatra, You Little Bimbo!
Death of a Party Animal
Downtown Doonesbury
Calling Dr. Whoopee
Talkin' About My G-G-Generation
We're Eating More Beets!
Read My Lips, Make My Day, Eat Quiche and Die!
Give Those Nymphs Some Hooters!
You're Smokin' Now, Mr. Butts!
I'd Go With the Helmet, Ray
Welcome to Club Scud!
What Is It, Tink, Is Pan in Trouble?

In Large Format

The Doonesbury Chronicles
Doonesbury's Greatest Hits
The People's Doonesbury
Doonesbury Dossier: The Reagan Years
Doonesbury Deluxe: Selected Glances Askance
Recycled Doonesbury: Second Thoughts on a Gilded Age

ACTION FIGURE!

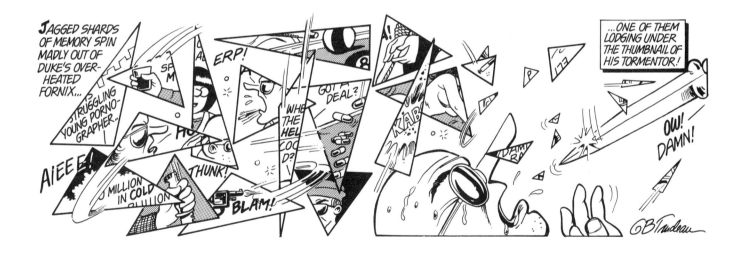

ANDREWS AND McMEEL · A UNIVERSAL PRESS SYNDICATE COMPANY · KANSAS CITY

DOONESBURY is distributed internationally by Universal Press Syndicate.

Action Figure! The Adventures of Doonesbury's Uncle Duke copyright © 1992 by G.B. Trudeau. All rights reserved. Printed in the United States of America. No part of this book may be used or reproduced in any manner whatsoever without written permission except in the case of reprints in the context of reviews. For information write Andrews and McMeel, a Universal Press Syndicate Company, 4900 Main Street, Kansas City, Missouri 64112.

ISBN: 0-8362-1702-0

Library of Congress Catalog Card Number: 92-72255

"Just waking up in the morning
means a lot to me."

— Keith Richards

19

HIT IT, MACARTHUR—THEY'RE BE-GINNING TO ARRIVE EN MASSE!

THE MOST HONORABLE TINA SLIMS, MINISTER OF WOMEN!

GOVERNOR! MAY I WELCOME YOU TO SAMOA!

YOU'RE BARKING UP THE WRONG TREE, HONEY. I'M MARRIED.

THE MOST HONORABLE ANTHONY HAYDEN-JONES, MINISTER OF SURFING AFFAIRS!

A REAL HONOR, SIR.

THANKS, TONY. SURF'S UP, I TRUST?

THE HONORABLE BOBBY VALDEZ, MINISTER OF MARIJUANA AND CENTRAL NER-VOUS SYSTEM DEPRESSANTS!

GOOD EVENING, MAN!

MACARTHUR, CANCEL MY APPOINTMENTS FOR TOMORROW!

EXCELLENCY, MACARTHUR TELLS ME YOU HAD A SPOT OF LAVA TROUBLE IN YOUR GARDEN LAST WEEK..

MORE LIKE A TOTAL WIPEOUT, TONY! WE GOT HIT SOMETHIN' FIERCE!

IT REALLY TICKED ME OFF! WE LOST EVERYTHING! — THE ROSES, THE PETUNIAS, THE BEGONIAS, SOME SENSATIONAL ORCHIDS AND AFRICAN VIOLETS THAT JUST KNOCKED YOUR EYES OUT!!

NOT TO MENTION A DAMN FINE GARDENER!

OH, REALLY? YOU LOST RALPHIE?

GOVERNOR, WE ALL THINK YOU'VE DONE A MARVELOUS JOB COPING WITH THE LATEST NATURAL DISASTERS!

WELL, IT'S BEEN NO PICNIC, I'LL TELL YOU THAT! YOU HAVE NO IDEA WHAT THE EMERGENCY RELIEF BUREAU-CRACY'S LIKE!

I MUST HAVE SPENT A WEEK PLEADING WITH THOSE MORONS IN WASHINGTON BEFORE THEY'D SEND ME AS MUCH AS A BAND-AID! EVERY LAST AGENCY IN TOWN'S ALL TIED UP WITH LOCAL DISASTERS!

DID YOU TRY THE PEACE CORPS?

SURE, I TRIED THE PEACE CORPS— I CABLED THEM SEVERAL TIMES!

AND?

THEY SENT ME A DOZEN MATH TEACHERS!

23

LOOK, BOY WONDER, YOU **CAN'T** TAKE ME OFF THE MASTHEAD! — MY READERS WILL HAVE YOUR **HEAD**!

WHAT READERS?! YOU HAVEN'T PRODUCED AN ARTICLE IN **YEARS**!

DUKE, IF YOU WANT TO STAY WITH THIS ORGANIZATION, YOU'RE GOING TO HAVE TO START PAYING SOME DUES AGAIN! I'M REASSIGNING YOU TO THE ROCK 'N' ROLL BEAT!

ROCK 'N' ROLL BEAT?! ARE YOU **MAD**!

YOUR FIRST PROJECT WILL BE AN UPDATE REPORT ON CHER.

A WRITER OF MY STATURE?!

CHER'S COOL — SHE WON'T MIND.

YOU'RE QUITE MAD, YOU KNOW. NO **WAY** I'M GOING TO COVER CHER!

YES, YOU ARE, DUKE! OR YOU DISAPPEAR FROM THE MASTHEAD FOR GOOD!

YOU **PUP**! YOU CAN'T **DO** THIS TO ME!

WHY? WHERE YOU GOING TO GO, DUKE — "LADIES HOME JOURNAL"?

DO YOU HAVE **ANY** IDEA WHAT EVEN A **TEMPORARY** GREGG AND CHER GIG COULD DO TO MY REP?

TEMPORARY? WHO SAID ANYTHING ABOUT TEMPORARY? I'M MAKING YOU BUREAU CHIEF!

GREGG AND CHER BUREAU CHIEF?!

AND I'M ONLY DOING IT BECAUSE WE'RE OLD FRIENDS.

WELL, DUKE, I'M SURE YOU'RE ANXIOUS TO MEET THE REST OF OUR CHER TASK FORCE!

CHER **WHAT**?!

MICHELLE HERE IS IN CHARGE OF THE MOBILE SURVEILLANCE UNITS... AND THAT'S ANNIE, WHO'S AN EXPERT ON CHER'S MEN. SHE ALSO CO-ORDINATES PAPARAZZI ACTIVITIES.

HI.

LESTER OVER THERE IS OUR INSIDE MAN..

INSIDE MAN?

YEAH — I'M A CLOSE PERSONAL FRIEND OF CHER'S DERMATOLOGIST.

WELL, I'M SURE YOU'VE GOT A LOT TO TALK ABOUT!

I'LL GET YOU FOR THIS..

WE GREW UP TOGETHER!

CHINA, MAC! HENRY'S ASKING ME TO GO TO CHINA!

REALLY?! WHAT A **WONDERFUL** OPPORTUNITY FOR YOU, SIR!

CHINA'S GOOD FORTUNE IS SAMOA'S MISFORTUNE, SIR. BUSH HAS BEEN RECALLED, AND THE PRESIDENT WANTS ME TO TAKE OVER AS **TOP ENVOY!**

I'VE BEEN DIRECTED TO APPEAR AT A SENATE CONFIRMATION HEARING NEXT MONTH..!

YOURS HAS BEEN A CAREER OF PUBLIC SERVICE WHICH SAMOANS WILL NOT SOON FORGET!

DO YOU THINK I SHOULD ACCEPT, MAC?

LET US NOT SAY ALOHA, SIR — BUT RATHER, AU REVOIR!

MAC, I THINK I'VE FIGURED OUT WHY THE PRESIDENT'S SENDING ME TO CHINA...

FORD'S TOUGHENING UP, SEE, PLAYING TO THE CONSERVATIVES! TO SHOW THAT HE'S NOT BEING DUPED BY THE REDS, HE'S SENDING A NO-NONSENSE CAREER DIPLOMAT TO PEKING TO INSURE THAT DETENTE IS A TWO-WAY STREET!

SOUNDS REASONABLE. BUT WHY YOU?

MY RECORD HERE, MAC — I'VE SHOWN I KNOW HOW TO WORK WITH MINORITIES!

"MINORITIES"?

AND THAT'S IMPORTANT, MAC— THOSE CHINESE ARE AN ESPECIALLY TRICKY PEOPLE!

THE IMPORTANT THING TO REMEMBER ABOUT THE CHINESE, MAC, IS THAT THEIR PRIMARY CONCERN IS USSR HEGEMONY.

THE CHINESE BELIEVE IN THE INEVITABILITY OF WAR WITH THE RUSKIES. BUT THEY ALSO HAVE AN ABIDING CONVICTION THAT THEY WILL PREVAIL!

THEIR POSITION IS SUMMED UP IN A POPULAR MAOIST SAYING: "THERE IS GREAT DISORDER UNDER HEAVEN AND THE SITUATION IS EXCELLENT."

SOUNDS LIKE ONE OF YOUR PARTIES, SIR.

YEAH, THAT'S WHY I THINK WE'RE GOING TO HIT IT OFF.

2 PEKING

1976-1977

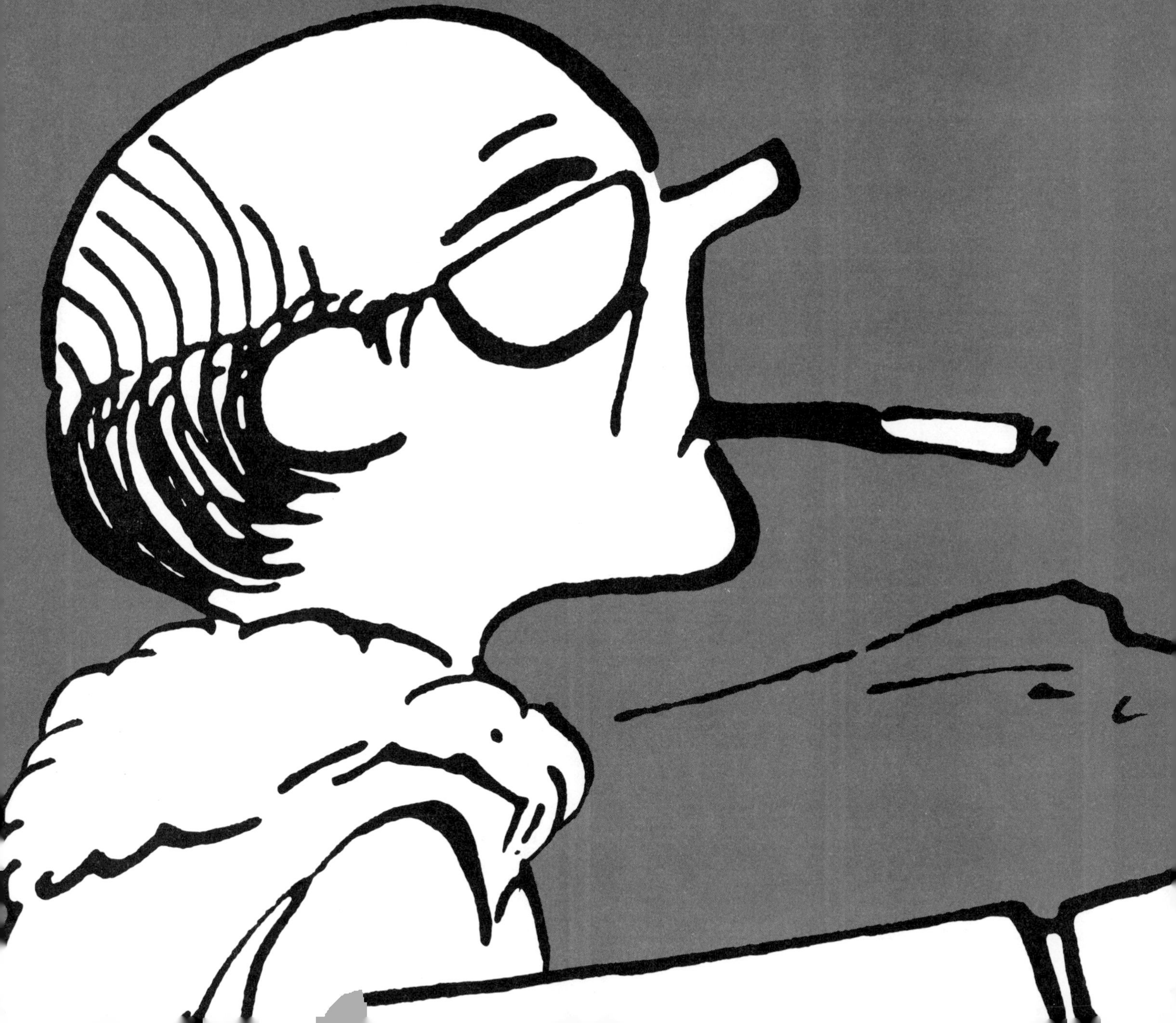

AS FAR AS DETENTE IS CONCERNED, WE'LL JUST HAVE TO SEE WHAT DEVELOPS. I'M SURE MY CHINESE HOSTS WOULD BE AS SADDENED TO SEE U.S. GUNBOATS STEAMING UP THE YANGTZE AS I WOULD BE.

SIR, DO YOU EXPECT TO CONTINUE INGESTING RECREATIONAL DRUGS DURING YOUR STAY IN CHINA?

ABSOLUTELY— I INTEND TO STRESS CONTINUITY IN MY PERSONAL HABITS!

I HAVE ALSO BEEN ASSURED BY MY ATTENDING MEDICAL OFFICER THAT HE'LL BE ABLE TO FILL THE PHARMACEUTICAL REQUIREMENTS OF THE LIAISON OFFICE SOCIAL FUNCTIONS.

BUT, SIR, AS YOU MUST KNOW, YOUR CHINESE HOSTS FROWN ON ALL FORMS OF EXCESS.

MY *CHINESE* HOSTS CAN GO SUCK EGGS.

A LIGHT DRIZZLE GREETED THE NEW CHIEF OF THE U.S. MISSION AS HIS PLANE TOUCHED DOWN HERE AT PEKING INTERNATIONAL AIRPORT..

THE PASSENGER DOOR OF THE AIRCRAFT HAS BEEN OPENED, AND CHINESE OFFICIALS ARE NOW GATHERING ON THE RUNWAY TO MEET THE NEW TOP ENVOY.

THE GREETING IS EXPECTED TO BE STRAINED, AS AMBASSADOR DUKE IS KNOWN TO BE OPENLY SUSPICIOUS OF HIS CHINESE HOSTS.

COVER ME— I THINK I CAN MAKE THE LIMO!

BUT, SIR— IT'S ONLY AN HONOR GUARD..

A FURTHER GOAL OF MINE IS THE SPEEDY IMPLEMENTATION OF NORMALIZATION.

(A FURTHER GOAL OF HIS IS THE SPEEDY IMPLEMENTATION OF NORMALIZATION.)

LASTLY, I COME TO CHINA IN THE HOPE OF FULFILLING A LIFE-LONG AMBITION — DROPPING ACID ON THE GREAT WALL.

(LASTLY, HE WISHES YOU GOOD HEALTH AND LONG LIFE.)

IN CONCLUSION, LET ME JUST SAY THAT I LOOK FORWARD TO A NEW SPIRIT OF CO-OPERATION FROM OUR CHINESE FRIENDS. I SINCERELY HOPE IT *WON'T* BE NECESSARY TO SHELL ANY PAGODAS.

(HE ALSO WISHES YOUR WIFE GOOD HEALTH.)

(THANK HIM, AND ASK HIM IF HE'D LIKE TO SEE THE GREAT WALL.)

45

"..AND BECAUSE MY CHINESE HOSTS WERE SO EAGER TO ORIENT ME, ENDLESS SIGHTSEEING BECAME MY MAJOR ACTIVITY."

"UNFORTUNATELY, THE GREATEST SIGHT OF ALL, THE CHAIRMAN HIMSELF, ELUDED ME FOR A SOLID MONTH. I BEGAN TO WONDER IF HE'D *EVER* SURFACE."

"THEN FINALLY LAST WEDNESDAY, AT 3:30 A.M., THE CALL CAME.."

HURRY, SIR—NO TIME TO WASTE!

ALRIGHT, ALRIGHT— JUST LET ME PUT MY PANTS ON, OKAY?!

TELL ME, HONEY—IS IT HARD TO CONVERSE WITH THE CHAIRMAN? I WAS TOLD HIS STROKE LEFT HIM WITH A SPEECH IMPAIRMENT..

YES, SIR. CHAIRMAN MAO HAS ALWAYS BEEN HARD TO UNDERSTAND BECAUSE HE SPEAKS AN OBSCURE RURAL DIALECT. AND NOW WITH THE STROKE, I SEEM TO BE THE ONLY TRANSLATOR WHO CAN STILL UNDERSTAND HIM.

NO KIDDING?.. MAN, THAT CERTAINLY LEAVES YOU WITH A HELL OF A RESPONSIBILITY, DOESN'T IT?

YES, SIR. IN A WAY, I'M SORT OF RUNNING THE COUNTRY.

I'LL KEEP THAT IN MIND.

..AND I BRING HIM GREETINGS FROM THE AMERICAN PEOPLE.

(AND HE BRINGS YOU GREETINGS FROM THE AMERICAN PEOPLE.)

(MMPHPH SPMUP LI MXZPQU!)

WHAT'D HE SAY?

THE CHAIRMAN SAYS IT GIVES HIM GREAT PLEASURE TO SEE HIS OLD FRIEND DAVID EISENHOWER AGAIN.

YOU MADE THAT UP, RIGHT? THINKING IT FUNNY?

I CALL THEM AS I HEAR THEM, SIR.

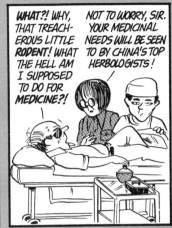

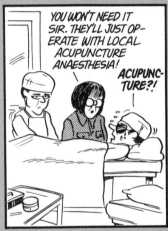

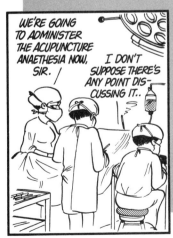

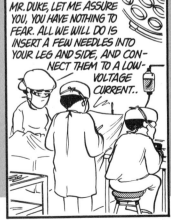

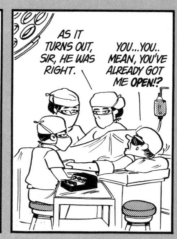
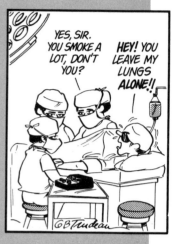

MR. DUKE, HAVE YOU STARTED YOUR SPEECH FOR TONIGHT'S BANQUET YET?

YEAH, HONEY, I GOT A FEW IDEAS DOWN. I'LL PROBABLY JUST WING IT, THOUGH.

IS THAT WISE, SIR? THE WHOLE CENTRAL COMMITTEE WILL BE IN ATTENDANCE.

LOOK, DON'T WORRY! IT'S JUST ANOTHER BANQUET GIG, HONEY!

I MEAN, I ACED THAT UNIVERSITY BANQUET DIDN'T I? YOU KNOW, WITH MY ADDRESS ON AMERICAN HUMOR?

I THOUGHT THOSE WERE POLISH JOKES, SIR.

YEAH, BUT THEY ORIGINATED IN THE STATES!

..AND I THANK MY CHINESE HOSTS FOR THEIR RELENTLESS HOSPITALITY!

(HE THANKS YOU FOR BEING HOSPITABLE.)

THE LAST YEAR HAS PASSED WITHOUT ANY MAJOR PROVOCATION AND I APPRECIATE THAT.

(HE THANKS YOU FOR BEING SO TOLERANT.)

I LOOK FORWARD TO MANY MORE YEARS OF WORKING WITH PEKING!

(HE DOESN'T KNOW YET HE'S BEING REPLACED BY LEONARD WOODCOCK.)

YOU'RE NOT PROJECTING, HONEY.

(HE DOESN'T KNOW YET HE'S BEING REPLACED BY LEONARD WOODCOCK!)

THERE'S BEEN A LOT OF TALK LATELY THAT JIMMY CARTER HAS BEEN IGNORING CHINA!

(HE BRINGS YOU GREETINGS FROM PRESIDENT CARTER!)

WELL, THERE'S A REASON FOR THAT! THE HUMAN RIGHTS SITUATION HERE IS SO BAD IT BOGGLES THE MIND!

(HE BRINGS GREETINGS FROM VICE-PRESIDENT MONDALE!)

CLAP! CLAP! CLAP! CLAP! CLAP! CLAP! CLAP!

WHY ARE THEY APPLAUDING, HONEY?

THEY LOVE YOU, SIR.

IT'S A SWEET LITTLE DEAL, NEPHEW! ABOUT AS TASTY A BUSINESS OPPORTUNITY AS I'VE EVER COME ACROSS!

100 ACRES OF THE RICHEST FARM LAND IN THE WHOLE SAN FERNANDO VALLEY! AND EACH ACRE JUST *THICK* WITH APRICOT TREES!

UH..DUKE, I'M SURE IT'S A GREAT DEAL, BUT FRANKLY, I CAN'T SEE YOU PURVEYING FRUIT!

FRUIT? WHO SAID ANYTHING ABOUT FRUIT? THE REAL PROFITS ARE IN THE PITS!

PITS?..OH, DUKE, NOT LAETRILE..

OF COURSE NOT. THAT WOULD BE ILLEGAL.

LAETRILE? YOU'RE GOING INTO THE *LAETRILE* BUSINESS?

BITE YOUR TONGUE, NEPHEW! OF *COURSE* NOT! LAETRILE'S STILL ILLEGAL IN THIS STATE!

ALL I'M DOING IS BUYING INTO A LITTLE APRICOT FARM! AND IF I JUST HAPPEN TO FIND A MARKET FOR MY PITS IN TIJUANA, WHO COULD BLAME ME FOR SELLING THEM?

UNCLE DUKE, THAT'S JUST AWFUL! HOW COULD YOU EVEN CONSIDER SUCH A SCHEME!

I SUPPOSE I WOULD BE REMISS IF I FAILED TO MENTION THE 600% PROFIT MARGIN.

DUKE, THE STUFF DOESN'T EVEN WORK ON *RATS!*

THEY'RE NOT BUYING. WHY DO YOU ALWAYS GET SO TICKED WHEN I THINK OF SOMETHING FIRST?

LOOK, I DON'T SEE WHAT YOU'RE GETTING SO WORKED UP ABOUT! IT'S NOT LIKE I'M GOING TO BE EXTRACTING THE LAETRILE MYSELF!

BESIDES, THIS APRICOT PLANTATION'S TOO GOOD A DEAL TO PASS UP! THE WHOLE SPREAD'S BEING LET GO FOR LESS THAN 300 BUCKS AN ACRE!

DUKE, WHO EXACTLY IS DOING THE LETTING GO?

FRIEND OF A FRIEND WHO'S FALLEN ON HARD TIMES! NAME'S TONY PLACEBO.

"PLACEBO"?

GUY'S HEARTBROKEN, OF COURSE, BUT BETTER ME THAN THE BANKS, YOU KNOW?

..AND ART BUCHWALD'S NOT AVAILABLE EITHER, WHICH MEANS WE'VE GOT ONLY *ONE* WEEK LEFT TO FIND SOMEONE TO GIVE THIS YEAR'S JOURNAL-ISM LECTURE!

ABE, I'VE GOT A SUGGESTION! HOW ABOUT FORMER AMBASSADOR DUKE, THE EX-GONZO STRINGER FOR "ROLLING STONE"?

HIS IS A UNIQUE PERSPECTIVE ON THE DARK UNDERSIDE OF OUTLAW JOURNALISM. AND HIS IMMENSE POPULARITY AMONG US KIDS WOULD LEND A CACHET TO THE LECTURE!

ACCORDING TO WHOM?

ZONKER. I'VE NEVER HEARD OF HIM MYSELF.

TRUST ME, GUYS. HE'D BE PERFECT! REALLY!

GOOD LORD, KID, IT'S ONLY SEVEN O'CLOCK! HAVEN'T YOU EVER HEARD OF TIME ZONES?

YES, SIR, I'M SORRY, SIR, BUT WE'RE KIND OF PRESSED. YOUR NEPHEW SAID IT WOULD BE OKAY TO CALL..

MY NEPHEW? ZONKER?

YES, SIR. HE'S ON THE SPEAKER'S COMMITTEE WITH ME..

LOOK, CHIEF, I DON'T GIVE A DAMN IF HE'S ON THE SAME..

AND HE SAID TO BE SURE TO MENTION THE $3,000. HONORARIUM TO YOU!

THAT RASCAL. HE REALLY SAID THAT?

YES, SIR. HE SEEMS TO THINK THE WORLD OF YOU.

MR. DUKE! MR. *DUKE!* OVER HERE, SIR!

HELLO?

I'M RONNIE, SIR! DID YOU HAVE A GOOD FLIGHT?

YEAH, IT WAS OKAY.

LET ME JUST SAY, SIR, HOW VERY HONORED WE ALL ARE THAT YOU WERE ABLE TO TAKE TIME FROM YOUR BUSY SCHEDULE TO COME SPEAK TO US!

UH-HUH. GOT MY FEE WITH YOU?

OH, YES, OF COURSE, SIR. IN TENS AND TWENTIES, AS REQUESTED.

..AND NOW, WITHOUT FURTHER ADO, THE PRINCE OF GONZO — AMBASSADOR **DUKE!**

YEAA! CLAP! CLAP! CLAP!

HE LOOKS A LITTLE SHAKY STILL, ZONKER..

THAT'S NORMAL. I JUST HOPE HE'S REASONABLY COHERENT!

GOOD EVENING. FEW OF NATURE'S WONDERS HAVE BEEN MORE WIDELY MISUNDERSTOOD THAN THE PLAYFUL PEYOTE BUTTON.

I THINK HE'S GOING TO BE OKAY..

MAY I HAVE THE FIRST SLIDE, PLEASE?

MR. DUKE, I'M THINKING OF BECOMING A REPORTER. WHAT ADVICE WOULD YOU GIVE SOMEONE WHO IS JUST STARTING OUT?

LOOK, JUNIOR, JOURNALISM IS A JUNGLE! NEVER FORGET THAT! IN JOURNALISM, THERE ARE NO WINNERS, JUST SURVIVORS! WE ARE TALKING SNAKE PIT CITY, SLIM!

SO DIG IT! I BEEN THERE! IF YOU FALTER FOR A **SECOND**, YOUR COLLEAGUES WILL **WASTE** YOU, WILL **SAVAGE** YOUR REP, YOUR NAME, YOUR.. YOUR..

WHAT WAS THE QUESTION AGAIN?

UM.. HOW DO YOU LIKE OUR CAMPUS?

ANY FURTHER QUERIES?

YES, MR. AMBASSADOR, WE MEMBERS OF THE AUDIENCE COULDN'T HELP NOTICING THAT YOU'RE STONED TO THE GILLS!

CONSIDERING YOUR SIZABLE LECTURE FEE, PAID IN PART BY CLASS DUES, CAN YOU THINK OF ANY REASON WHY WE SHOULDN'T BE GROSSLY INSULTED?

PSST! DUKE! YOUR MOM!

LOOK, I WAS HOPING TO AVOID THE SUBJECT OF MOTHER'S TUMOR, BUT..

GOOD NEWS, UNCLE DUKE?

YOU BET IT IS, NEPHEW! OL' MAN WILLIAMS WANTS TO INTERVIEW ME FOR THE REDSKINS MANAGER POSITION!

YOU? HOW COME?

WELL, HE CHECKED OUT MY RESUME AND CLIPPINGS FROM MY SPORTS WRITING DAYS..

AMONG OTHER THINGS, IT SEEMS HE WAS QUITE IMPRESSED WITH MY DETAILED KNOWLEDGE OF THE NEW WORK THAT'S BEING DONE WITH HIGH-PERFORMANCE STEROIDS!

A MANAGER NEEDS TO KNOW THAT?

OH, ABSOLUTELY! WHY DO YOU THINK HE HAD TO LET GEORGE ALLEN GO?

MR. DUKE, I THINK YOU'RE QUITE MISTAKEN ABOUT THE EXTENT OF THE PILL PROBLEM. WHY, NFL OFFICIALS GIVE ANTI-DRUG LECTURES EVERY MONTH..

YEAH, AND 90% OF YOUR PLAYERS ARE LAUGHING THEIR JOCKS OFF THE WHOLE TIME!

MR. WILLIAMS, YOUR PLAYERS AREN'T PILLHEADS BECAUSE THEY **WANT** TO BE. HELL, NOBODY **LIKES** TAKING PILLS! THEY TAKE 'EM BECAUSE THEY'RE CONCERNED ABOUT WHAT THE NEXT ATHLETE MIGHT BE DOING!

OH.. OH, I SEE.

IT'S A REAL PROBLEM, SIR! AND I'LL TELL YOU, SOMETIMES IT JUST BREAKS MY HEART TO SEE IT!

BUT YOU SAY YOU'VE HAD SOME EXPERIENCE IN THIS AREA?

I'VE BEEN AROUND THE TRACK A FEW TIMES, YES.

MR. WILLIAMS, I HOPE I'M NOT BEING OUT OF LINE IN TELLING YOU THAT I THINK I UNDERSTAND YOUR PROBLEM. BASICALLY, YOU'RE HOT FOR THE SUPER BOWL!

CAN YOU GET ME THERE, MR. DUKE?

WITH TIME? WITHOUT QUESTION, SIR! BUT I'D BE REMISS IF I FAILED TO MENTION THAT MY TALENTS ARE IN CONSIDERABLE DEMAND NOW!

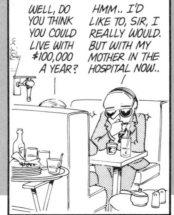

WELL, DO YOU THINK YOU COULD LIVE WITH $100,000 A YEAR?

HMM.. I'D LIKE TO, SIR, I REALLY WOULD. BUT WITH MY MOTHER IN THE HOSPITAL NOW..

PITY. COULD YOU SUGGEST ANYONE ELSE WHO..

OH, THE HECK WITH MOM! THIS IS TOO IMPORTANT!

".. AND WE IN THE FRONT OFFICE OFFER MR. DUKE OUR WARMEST WELCOME TO THE REDSKINS ORGANIZATION!" ..OKAY, WE'LL TAKE QUESTIONS NOW..

MR. DUKE, AS FAR AS WE CAN TELL, YOU BRING NO RELEVANT EXPERIENCE TO YOUR JOB. COULD YOU COMMENT?

YEAH. THAT'S A COMPLETE BUNCH OF GARBAGE.

BESIDES MY RECORD IN ADMINISTRATION, I BRING TO MY JOB AN AWESOME EXPERTISE IN SPORTS MEDICINE. IT WILL BE MY DUTY TO SEE THAT EACH AND EVERY MAN IS SAFELY WIRED BEFORE HE GOES OUT ON THAT BALL FIELD!

WHAT? YOU MEAN YOU'LL ACTUALLY BE DISPENSING PILLS?

YES. MY CONTRACT EXPLICITLY..

THANKS FOR COMING, BOYS!

DUKE, THERE'S NO WAY WE'RE GONNA GET ANY OF THESE KIDS! THE BEST OF THEM WILL BE ALL GONE BY ROUND SEVEN.

SEVEN? WE CAN'T MAKE A PICK UNTIL ROUND SEVEN?

THAT'S RIGHT. OUR TOP DRAFT CHOICES HAVE BEEN LONG SINCE TRADED AWAY..

A **POX** ON GEORGE ALLEN! NO WONDER THE TALENTLESS TOAD BOLTED TOWN WHEN HE DID!

TELL ME ABOUT IT. THIS IS THE THIRD YEAR I'VE HAD TO JUNK MY SCOUTING REPORTS!

I JUST DON'T SEE HOW HE GOT AWAY WITH THAT "THE FUTURE IS NOW" GARBAGE AS LONG AS HE DID!

I GUESS BECAUSE NOBODY ELSE HERE UNDERSTOOD POETRY.

YEAH, WELL, THINGS ARE GOING TO CHANGE AROUND HERE!

WELL, DUKE, IF WE CAN'T DRAFT, WE MIGHT AS WELL GO SHOPPING. GOT ANY FREE AGENTS YOU LIKE?

YEAH, HOW ABOUT "LAVA-LAVA" LENNY? YOU FAMILIAR WITH "LAVA-LAVA'S" WORK?

NOPE. WHO IS HE?

A KID I DISCOVERED SLINGING COCONUTS DURING MY TENURE IN PAGO PAGO. HE'S NOW PLAYING FRONT FOUR FOR THE LIONS.

ALL FRONT FOUR? SOUNDS LIKE A BIG BOY..

BIG? BOBBY, THE OPPOSITION'S LUCKY IF IT EVEN GETS A **GLIMPSE** OF THE QUARTERBACK!

UH-HUH..

I'M NOT KIDDING! WHEN I FIRST SAW HIM IN SAMOA, I THOUGHT HE WAS AN OFFSHORE ISLAND!

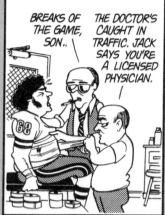

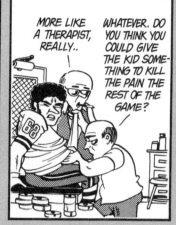

Panel 1: TIME OUT! / OH, NO, EDDIE! NOT AGAIN!

Panel 2: THAT'S THE SECOND QUARTERBACK IN A ROW THAT HE'S CLOTHESLINED! HE'S GOING TO KILL US WITH PENALTIES!

Panel 3: DUKE, WHATEVER YOU FED THAT KID WAS WAY THE HELL OUT OF LINE! / I'M SORRY, COACH. I MUST HAVE MISCALCULATED THE DOSAGE..

Panel 4: OH, MY GOD! HE'S GOING AFTER THE REF! / GO FETCH MY DART GUN, BOY.

Panel 5: SO HOW'S EDDIE DOING, KID? / HE'S OUT FOR THE SEASON. AS ARE BOTH OF THE GUYS HE CLOTHESLINED.

Panel 6: SIR, I MAY BE A LITTLE OLD-FASHIONED, BUT ALL THESE OVER-AMPED PLAYERS BASHING EACH OTHER'S BRAINS OUT.. CAN THAT BE GOOD FOR THE GAME?

Panel 7: IT'S THE OWNERS, SON. THEY'RE BLIND TO THE PROBLEM. WITHOUT URINE TESTS, WHAT CAN I DO? / I DON'T KNOW, SIR, BUT RIGHT NOW YOU'RE PUTTING A LOT OF GUYS IN THE HOSPITAL!

Panel 8: HEY, LOOK, CHOIR BOY.. / SIR, I'VE DECIDED TO GO TO THE PAPERS.

Panel 9: GO TO THE PAPERS? ARE YOU MAD, KID? YOU WANT TO GET THE WHOLE FRONT OFFICE BUSTED? / WELL, NO, SIR, BUT I JUST CAN'T SIT BY AND WATCH THE GAME RUINED BY HOMICIDAL SPEED-FREAKS!

Panel 10: LOOK, RILEY! THIS IS FOOTBALL! TO QUOTE HARRY TRUMAN, IF YOU CAN'T TAKE THE HEAT, THEN GET THE HELL OUT OF NAGASAKI! / YOU LETTING ME GO, SIR?

Panel 11: WELL, NOW THAT YOU MENTION IT, THAT'S A DAMN GOOD.. / "BOY, 15, AXED BY REDSKINS' DRUG DOC."

Panel 12: SIT DOWN, RILEY.. / IT'S TOO LATE FOR THAT, SIR.

CLACKITY! RUUMMBLE! CLACKITY! WHIPPITY! WHIP!

EXTRA! INSIDER, 15, RAPS 'SKINS IN SPEED SCANDAL!

Post

shington Post

SPORTS
MONDA

DrugDoc Termed 'Menace To Sport'
By Richard Redfern

WASHINGTON— An Int amphetamine scandal-ρ drus

neral Manager Duke .000 Injuries ρ today with

INS 78

RING! RING!

GET THAT, WILL YA, KID?

I WONDER IF WE COULD TALK FIRST, SIR..

GBTrudeau

IT'S ALL THERE, DUKE—THE DRUGS, THE INJURIES, EVERYTHING! MY PHONE HASN'T STOPPED RING-ING SINCE THE EARLY EDI-TION HIT THE STREETS!

DAMN! THIS COULD BE WORSE THAN THE STOLEN PLAYBOOK! HOW THE HELL DID THE "POST" FIND OUT, COACH? EDDIE'S THE ONLY ONE BESIDES US WHO KNOWS ABOUT IT, AND HE'S IN A COMA!

I DON'T KNOW, DUKE, BUT IF YOU DON'T TRACK THE LITTLE SNITCH DOWN FAST, YOU MIGHT AS WELL START PACKING!

TROUBLE, SIR?

IT JUST CAME TO ME, COACH.

IT WASN'T MY FAULT, SIR. THEY PLIED ME WITH CHEESEBURGERS.

GBTrudeau

YOUR FOOTBALL ARTICLE SEEMS TO BE CAUSING QUITE A STIR, RICHARD..

YEAH, THAT GUY DUKE SURE DOESN'T TAKE THINGS LYING DOWN.

HE RELEASED A 2,000 WORD REBUTTAL YESTERDAY, AND TODAY HE'S HOLDING A PRESS CONFERENCE IN HIS OFFICE ..

HE CLAIMS HE'S EVEN GOING TO PRODUCE THE INJURED PLAYER TO TESTIFY ON HIS BEHALF!

I DUNNO, SIR, HE DOESN'T LOOK SO GOOD..

NURSE! CUT THIS MAN DOWN!

GBTrudeau

..AND DESPITE MY HEATED PRO-TESTATIONS, EDDIE HAS CRAWLED FROM HIS HOSPITAL BED TO JOIN ME IN OUTRAGED DENIAL OF THIS ALLEGED PIECE OF REPORTING!

THIS ARTICLE REPRESENTS THE SHODDIEST KIND OF JOURNALISM! NAMES, DATES, PLACES ARE **ALL** INACCURATE! EVEN DOSAGES ARE DISTORTED AND TAKEN TOTALLY OUT OF CONTEXT!

AS EDDIE VIGOROUSLY CONFIRMS, THE "CONTROLLED SUBSTANCES" I GAVE HIM IN LAST SUNDAY'S GAME WERE NOTHING MORE THAN COMMON ASPIRIN TABLETS! RIGHT, EDDIE?

MMPHH.

NOW, I HOPE WE'VE HEARD THE LAST OF THIS SILLY EPISODE!

G B Trudeau

>WHEEZE! COUGH! COUGH!

WHILE WE'RE ALL HERE, I'D LIKE TO TAKE THE OPPORTUN-ITY TO COMMENT FURTHER ON RED-FERN'S INFLAMMATORY PROSE..

UNNHH..

IT IS A SORRY STATE OF AFFAIRS WHEN A POLITI-CAL REPORTER IS SENT TO COVER FOOTBALL, A SUB-JECT HE IS CLEARLY UN-EQUIPPED TO COMMENT ON!

UNNH.. ARRGH!

OBVIOUSLY, IN FOOTBALL PEOPLE GET HURT! BUT IT IS THE RISK OF INJURY THAT MAKES THE GAME GREAT! IT IS THE COURAGE OF ATH-LETES AS THEY..

BONK!

EDDIE, WILL YOU SETTLE DOWN? THIS IS IMPORTANT.

G B Trudeau

HEY, BOSS! WHAT ARE YOU **DOING?** YOU'RE DUE AT A RECEPTION IN TEN MINUTES!

RECEP-TION? WHAT RECEPTION?

FOR THE CHINESE FOREIGN EXCHANGE STUDENTS! YOU AC-CEPTED **WEEKS** AGO!

OUT OF THE QUESTION, RILEY! CAN'T YOU SEE I'M BUSY?

BUSY? DOING WHAT?

I FORGET. CHECK MY APPOINTMENT BOOK.

"11:30 TO 4:00, FIELD TRIP TO FRONTAL LOBES.."

THAT'S IT! I LEFT AN HOUR AGO!

G B Trudeau

WELL! THE STUDENTS CERTAINLY SEEM TO BE FASCINATED BY YOUR MR. DUKE!

UH-HUH. SAY, WHO'S THE YOUNG LADY WHO HAS BEEN MONOPOLIZING HIM?

THAT'S MS. HUAN. SHE'S FROM PEKING.

ACCORDING TO HER, SHE AND MR. DUKE WERE CLOSE FRIENDS DURING HIS TOUR OF DUTY IN CHINA..

WILL YOU BE SHOWING ME WASHINGTON BY NIGHT, SIR?

CAN'T MAKE ANY SUDDEN MOVES.. HAVE TO STAY CALM..

EXCUSE ME, SIRS. I WONDER IF YOU COULD TELL ME WHERE I MIGHT FIND MR. DUKE..

SHOULD BE IN THE CLUBHOUSE, MISS. FIRST DOOR ON THE RIGHT.

THANK YOU.

NOT AT ALL.

MAY I JUST SAY YOU'RE QUITE A PAIR OF SPECIMENS, SIRS.

PART OF THE JOB, MISS.

YOU SHOULD SEE THE GUYS WHO START.

THERE YOU ARE, SIR!

OH, NO..

I'VE BEEN LOOKING ALL OVER FOR YOU! I'VE JUST BEEN TALKING TO YOUR RESERVE QUARTERBACK! WHAT A GREAT GUY!

THIS BETTER BE AN AFTER-EFFECT..

LISTEN, I THINK YOU SHOULD PLAY HIM. HE'S MUCH BETTER LOOKING THAN THE GUY YOU GOT PLAYING NOW.

USED TO BE A TIME WHEN YOU KNEW WHAT WENT INTO THIS STUFF..

UM.. YOU'RE NOT GOING TO CHANGE FOR OUR DATE, SIR?

THAT DOES IT! I'M SWITCHING PHARMACISTS!

89

"THE NATIONAL RIFLE ASSOCIATION THEREFORE OPPOSES ANY AND ALL LEGISLATIVE ATTEMPTS TO CONTROL OUR CONSTITUTIONAL RIGHT TO BEAR ARMS!"

THAT'S THE END OF OUR PREPARED STATEMENT, MR. CHAIRMAN. I'D BE HAPPY TO ENTERTAIN ANY QUESTIONS.

MR. DUKE, DOES YOUR GROUP'S OPPOSITION EXTEND TO A SIMPLE REQUIREMENT OF SERIAL NUMBERS TO AID POLICE IN IDENTIFICATION?

WHAT'S WRONG WITH DENTAL RECORDS?

I WAS REFERRING TO THE GUNS.

SENATOR, THE POINT IS THAT ONCE YOU HAVE GUN CONTROL, THE ONLY PEOPLE LEFT WITH GUNS ARE CRIMINALS!

WHICH WOULD PREVENT A **GREAT** MANY MURDERS, MR. DUKE!

AS YOU WELL KNOW, ALMOST 70% OF ALL MURDERS ARE COMMITTED AMONG FAMILY MEMBERS OR FRIENDS. AND OVER HALF OF THEM INVOLVE HANDGUNS!

EXACTLY! SO LOOK AT IT FROM THE POINT OF VIEW OF THE VICTIM! WHAT IF **YOUR** WIFE WERE ATTACKING YOU WITH A HANDGUN?

I DON'T FOLLOW, MR. DUKE.

WELL, WOULDN'T YOU WANT TO BE IN A POSITION TO RETURN THE FIRE?

WELL, I..UH..

YOU DON'T HAVE TO ANSWER THAT, JIM.

THE QUESTION WE ARE FACING, THEN, MR. DUKE, IS WHETHER THE WISHES OF 80% OF THE AMERICAN PEOPLE WILL AGAIN GO UNHEEDED..

I CANNOT SPEAK FOR MY COLLEAGUES, BUT I FOR ONE AM **FED UP** WITH YOUR DEADLY LOBBY AND ITS FANATICAL DEFENSE OF A TRAGIC AND UNCONSCIONABLE PUBLIC POLICY!

I SEE.

SHALL I PUT YOU DOWN FOR A MILLION POST CARDS, THEN, SENATOR?

DON'T TRY TO INTIMIDATE **ME**, MR. DUKE!

TEHERAN

5

1979-1981

PARACHUTE? ME? ARE YOU MAD, ANDREWS? A SMALL RISK CONSIDERING THE STAKES, DUKE..

MAY I JUST REMIND YOU THAT AT THIS POINT, THE ONLY THING STANDING BETWEEN OUR WHOLE WAY OF LIFE AND ARMAGEDDON IS ONE 42-YEAR-OLD BALDING BAGMAN—YOU!

ANDREWS, HAVE YOU EVER HURLED YOURSELF OUT OF AN AIRPLANE AT 30,000 FEET? IT'S PERFECTLY SAFE, DUKE. BESIDES, THE IRANIAN AIR FORCE ALMOST NEVER PATROLS AT NIGHT.

NIGHT? HOW AM I SUPPOSED TO FIND THE DAMN TARGET AT **NIGHT?** YOU JUST FOLLOW THE TRACERS. LOOK, DUKE, I'D DO IT MYSELF IF IT WEREN'T FOR MY BACK.

WELL? THEY LEFT ANKARA ON TIME, "MOTHER." "EAGLE" SHOULD HAVE LANDED IN IRAN NEARLY TWO HOURS AGO.

DAMN HIM! DUKE KNOWS HE'S SUPPOSED TO CONTACT US ON TOUCHDOWN! MAYBE HIS PARACHUTE DIDN'T OPEN, SIR.

NOT A CHANCE. I PACKED IT MYSELF. WELL, MAYBE HE DECIDED TO KEEP THE PAYOFF MONEY FOR HIMSELF.

PERHAPS. I WAS HOPING HIS MOTHER WOULD DISCOURAGE THAT. THAT REMINDS ME. I BETTER CHECK ON HER AIR SUPPLY.

SORRY, "MOTHER," NO WORD FROM "EAGLE" YET. DAMN! THERE'S GOING TO BE HELL TO PAY AT THE NEXT BOARD MEETING FOR THIS!

IF THEY'VE GOT "EAGLE," WE'VE LOST "DIPSTICK," COMPROMISED OUR LIBYAN SPOT MARKET OPERATIVES, AND PROBABLY EXPOSED THE KUWAIT PAYOFFS! WE'RE STARING AT A MILLION BARREL SHORTFALL!

OH.

WHATEVER HAPPENED TO EXPLORATORY DRILLING? TOO RISKY. YOU DON'T SUPPOSE "EAGLE" WAS TOO STONED TO PULL HIS CORD, DO YOU?

"MOTHER"! A CABLE FROM TEHERAN!

FINALLY! GIVE IT HERE!

"REGRET TO INFORM YOU EAGLE HAS BOMBED. DIPSTICK."

MOTHER OF ALLAH! THEY CAUGHT HIM ALREADY?

GOD HELP US ALL.

A TOURIST? WITH OVER $200,000 IN CASH?

SO I'M NOT KARL MALDEN. SUE ME.

GOOD EVENING. TODAY FORMER UNITED STATES AMBASSADOR DUKE WAS CAPTURED WHILE PARACHUTING INTO THE AHVAZ OIL FIELDS IN IRAN. ROLAND HEDLEY HAS DETAILS.

THE REVOLUTIONARY GOVERNMENT OF THE AYATOLLAH KHOMEINI ANNOUNCED TONIGHT THAT THE ONETIME WASHINGTON REDSKINS FIELD GENERAL WOULD BE TRIED AND CONVICTED OF HIGH CRIMES AGAINST GOD.

ALTHOUGH DUE PROCESS AS PRACTICED IN THE WEST IS VIRTUALLY UNKNOWN HERE, ABC NEWS HAS LEARNED THAT AMBASSADOR DUKE WAS PERMITTED THE CUSTOMARY PHONE CALL..

HEY, MAN, THOSE ARE THE BREAKS.

DAMMIT, BRENNER! I NEED THOSE KRUGGERRANDS!

THIS IS ROLAND HEDLEY. IT'S A BLEAK, DARK MORNING HERE IN TEHERAN AS THE ESPIONAGE TRIAL OF FORMER AMBASSADOR DUKE GETS UNDER WAY!

IN THE NEW IRAN, THE ISLAMIC KANGAROO COURTS ARE CUSTOMARILY GAVELED TO ORDER AT AN UNGODLY 4:00 A.M.! TODAY SHOULD BE NO EXCEPTION.

TENSION HAS BEEN MOUNTING HERE ALL WEEK AS..

THE WHOLE WORLD IS WATCHING! THE WHOLE WORLD IS WATCHING!

AH, HERE COMES THE DEFENDANT NOW!

THE WHOLE.. THUD! UNH!

MR. DUKE WAS THEN DRAGGED SCREAMING AND KICKING TO THE GRAVEL ROOFTOP OF THE COURTHOUSE, A POPULAR SPOT IN RECENT MONTHS FOR DISCIPLINING FORMER SAVAK AGENTS.

AS YET, HOWEVER, THERE HAS BEEN NO OFFICIAL INDICATION THAT THE SENTENCE HAS BEEN CARRIED OUT. CERTAINLY THIS REPORTER HAS HEARD NO SHOTS, AND HE HAS KEPT HIS EARS PRICKED.

MOREOVER, THERE ARE NOW REPORTS THAT SENSITIVE NEGOTIATIONS MAY BE UNDER WAY IN A LAST-DITCH ATTEMPT TO SAVE THE FORMER AMBASSADOR'S LIFE.

$500,000! IN GOLD!

$250,000! AND THAT'S MY FINAL OFFER!

WHAT'S IT SAY, ZONK?

"REGRET TO INFORM YOU YOUR UNCLE DUKE HAS BEEN DECLARED LEGALLY DEAD."

"READING OF WILL SCHEDULED FOR MONDAY. PLEASE COME SOONEST TO HELP ORGANIZE PERSONAL EFFECTS. CONDOLENCES. T. BANNON, ATTORNEY-AT-LAW."

GEE... WHO DO YOU SUPPOSE MOVED TO HAVE HIM DECLARED LEGALLY DEAD?

I'M NOT SURE, BUT I'VE GOT A PRETTY GOOD IDEA!

YOU WANT THE STEREO PACKED TOO, BUDDY?

NO, NO, JUST PUT IT IN THE BACK OF MY VAN.

THIS SIDE UP

FRAGILE

IS THAT YOU, BRENNER?

HEY, ZONK! GOOD TO SEE YOU AGAIN, MAN!

DUKE

BRENNER, WHAT THE HELL IS GOING ON? WHO HAD DUKE DECLARED DEAD?

IT HAD TO BE DONE SOONER OR LATER, MAN. LIFE GOES ON, YOU KNOW?

DUKE

SO YOU WROTE HIM OFF? JUST LIKE THAT?

WELL, WE WERE THINKING OF A MEMORIAL SERVICE, BUT HIS ATTORNEY AND I FIGURED WE OUGHTA TRY TO KEEP EXPENSES DOWN.

DUKE

AS A COURTESY TO HIS HEIRS, NO DOUBT.

RIGHT. BESIDES, I COULDN'T REMEMBER WHICH CULT HE BELONGED TO.

DUKE

GLAD YOU GOT HERE SO FAST, ZONK. THERE'S A LOT OF STUFF TO SORT THROUGH BEFORE THE WILL READING!

WHO'S COMING TO THE READING, BRENNER?

A PRETTY HEAVY CROWD, MAN. A GANG OF CREDITORS, A COUPLE IRS GUYS, AND A U.S. MARSHAL.

A U.S. MARSHAL?

NOT TO WORRY, MAN. I CHECKED IT OUT, AND MOST OF DUKE'S ESTATE IS INADMISSIBLE.

IMAGINE MY RELIEF.

ALL WE GOTTA DO IS GET THE SERIAL NUMBERS OFF.

FIND ANYTHING INTERESTING YET, MAN?

ARE YOU KIDDING? JUST LOOK AT ALL THIS STUFF!

PARKING TICKETS, EVICTION NOTICES, BETTING STUBS, FOOD STAMPS, BOUNCED CHECKS, REJECTION SLIPS, UNFINISHED MANUSCRIPTS, OVERDUE BILLS..

.. PRESCRIPTION BLANKS, FORGED PASSPORTS.. WHY, BRENNER, THERE'S A RECORD OF FAILURE AND MALFEASANCE HERE THAT SPANS OVER TWENTY YEARS!

YOU THINKING OF EDITING HIS PAPERS, MAN?

I DON'T KNOW IF I COULD DO IT JUSTICE!

DID YOU KNOW DUKE STARTED KEEPING JOURNALS A FEW YEARS BACK, BRENNER?

NO KIDDING, MAN? DOES HE MENTION ME IN THEM?

SURE, RIGHT AT THE TOP. "JAN. 13, 1975. APPOINTMENT TO SAMOA CAME THROUGH. AM CELEBRATING WITH PART OF BRENNER'S NEW SHIPMENT OF AMYLS.."

OH, WOW..

"I'M ON MY FIFTH TAB AND IT LOOKS LIKE I'VE BEEN RIPPED OFF AGAIN. THIS STUFF IS SO BAD I'M NOT EVEN SLIGHTLY BIFFLE DINKED!"

HEE, HEE!

"IF THAT LEBBLE BIFFDECKER SNIT FIDDLE-GANG, WHIMSICK RIPPIZ LUNGS OUT."

HE ALMOST DID, TOO.

"JAN. 16, 1975, PAGO PAGO. ARRIVED TODAY TO SERVE IN MY CAPACITY AS NEWLY APPOINTED GOVERNOR OF AMERICAN SAMOA."

"RECEPTION WAS MAGNIFICENT. GREETED BY 21-GUN SALUTE, AND MY NEW AIDE-DE-CAMP, MACARTHUR, PRESENTED ME WITH A SILVER THERMOS OF DAIQUIRIS."

"HAVE TAKEN INSTANT LIKING TO SAMOAN PEOPLE, ESPECIALLY STAFF AT GOVERNOR'S MANSION. THEY ARE GENTLE, WARM, AND POSSESSED OF AN ALMOST CHILDLIKE INNOCENCE."

"JAN. 17. HONEYMOON OVER. FOUND SEED IN ORANGE JUICE. HAD COOK FLOGGED."

"JULY 1, 1975. THIS MORNING AT 3 A.M., PAGO PAGO SLAMMED TWICE BY MASSIVE TIDAL WAVE."

"HAVE EXTENDED STATE OF EMERGENCY DECLARED AFTER TYPHOON. ALSO IMPOSING MARTIAL LAW TO KEEP STREETS FREE OF LOOTERS."

"CURRENTLY SUFFERING FROM SEVERE SHORTAGES OF FOOD, FRESH WATER, MEDICAL SUPPLIES AND ENGLISH TEACHERS. CHOLERA EPIDEMIC ALSO SEEMS IMMINENT."

"JULY 3. SITUATION HOPELESS. OFF FOR WIMBLEDON FINALS."

"APRIL 15, 1976. PEKING. INTENSE NEGOTIATIONS ON STATUS OF U.S./CHINA RELATIONS CONTINUE AT GREAT HALL OF THE PEOPLE.."

"TENG IS UNCOMPROMISING ON TAIWAN ISSUE. I MAKE NINE SEPARATE PROPOSALS, INCLUDING GENEROUS CASH SETTLEMENTS, PLUS POINTS. AM REBUKED AT EVERY TURN."

"APRIL 16. TENG REMAINS INTRACTABLE. IN ATTEMPT TO BREAK DEADLOCK, I CALL IN AIR STRIKES ON IMPERIAL PALACE."

"APRIL 17. PENTAGON OVERRULES STRIKES. AM LOSING FACE."

OKAY, IF EVERYONE HAS SOMETHING TO DRINK, I'D LIKE TO GET THIS SHOW ON THE ROAD.

I'M T.F. BANNON, COUNSEL FOR THE FIRM OF TORTS, TARTZ AND TORQUE, AND PERSONAL ATTORNEY FOR AMBASSADOR DUKE.

IT IS MY UNHAPPY TASK TO BE HERE TODAY TO READ THE WILL OF MR. DUKE, WHO IS.. UH.. PRESUMED DEAD AT THIS TIME.

STILL NO WORD FROM THE DECEASED YET, RIGHT?

NOT A PEEP, MAN. LET'S DO IT.

YOU A FRIEND OF THE FAMILY?

YOU MIGHT SAY THAT I WORK FOR THE INTERNAL REVENUE SERVICE.

REALLY? HAVE YOU KNOWN DUKE LONG?

I WAS FIRST ASSIGNED TO HIS CASE IN 1963.

WOW..

HOW YOU BEARING UP?

NOT SO GOOD. IT'S SORT OF THE END OF AN ERA.

.."AND BEING OF ACCEPTABLY SOUND MIND AND WILL, I HEREBY LEAVE MY ENTIRE ESTATE TO.."

.."MY BELOVED PROTEGE, MR. ZONKER HARRIS."

HUH?

OH, WOW..

YOU WERE HIS FAVORITE DEALER, I TAKE IT.

NO, NO, I'M AS SURPRISED AS YOU ARE!

104

GOOD EVENING. THERE WAS ANOTHER DRAMATIC BREAKTHROUGH TODAY IN THE CONTINUING SAGA OF THE AMERICAN HOSTAGES.

THE STATE DEPARTMENT HAS FORMALLY ANNOUNCED THAT NEGOTIATIONS HAVE JUST BEEN COMPLETED FOR THE RELEASE OF AN ADDITIONAL, 53RD HOSTAGE.

THE HOSTAGE'S IDENTITY IS STILL NOT KNOWN, BUT HE IS BEING REFERRED TO BY IRANIAN SOURCES AS "THE BALD SPY."

THE WHAT?

YOU KNOW A BALD SPY?

..AND SOURCES SAY THE 53RD HOSTAGE, KNOWN ONLY AS "THE BALD SPY," WILL BE FREE WITHIN HOURS.

NEGOTIATIONS FOR THE MYSTERY HOSTAGE'S RELEASE WERE SAID TO HAVE BEEN DIFFICULT, INVOLVING SEVERAL HOURS OF HAGGLING OVER EXACT TERMS.

A BREAKTHROUGH WAS FINALLY REACHED LATE LAST NIGHT WHEN U.S. OFFICIALS AGREED TO UNFREEZE ADDITIONAL IRANIAN ASSETS TOTALLING $300.

HOW MUCH?

IT WAS THE BEST WE COULD DO, BALD ONE.

GOOD EVENING. TODAY THE IDENTITY OF THE 53RD HOSTAGE WAS MADE KNOWN. HE IS FORMER U.S. AMBASSADOR DUKE..

I KNEW IT! I KNEW IT WAS UNCLE DUKE!

AT THE TEHERAN AIRPORT THIS MORNING, HE SPOKE WITH REPORTERS..

MR. DUKE, HOW DOES IT FEEL TO BE FREE?

GREAT. AND I WANT TO THANK THE THOUSANDS OF PEOPLE AROUND THE WORLD WHO PRESSURED IRAN FOR MY RELEASE. I'M CERTAIN THAT PUBLIC OUTRAGE WAS THE ONLY THING THAT STOOD BETWEEN ME AND A BRUTAL DEATH!

UH.. BUT NOBODY KNEW YOU WERE A HOSTAGE, SIR..

BALONEY. THERE WAS INTERNATIONAL PRESSURE. I COULD FEEL IT.

DOCTOR, WHAT SORT OF CONDITION IS THE 53RD HOSTAGE IN?

PHYSICALLY, HE SEEMS TO BE FINE..

PSYCHOLOGICALLY, THERE APPEAR TO BE SOME PROBLEMS. WHAT IS NOT CLEAR, HOWEVER, IS HOW MANY OF THEM EXISTED PRIOR TO HIS CAPTIVITY.

DOC, HAS HE CALLED HIS FAMILY YET?

AS A MATTER OF FACT, I THINK HE WAS PLANNING ON PHONING HIS LOVED ONES THIS MORNING..

$1000 ON OAKLAND, GOT IT?

DUKE, THE GAME WAS TWO WEEKS AGO. WHERE YOU BEEN?

BRENNER? IS THAT YOU?

DUKE?.. YOU'RE.. YOU'RE ALIVE!

SORRY TO DISAPPOINT YOU, BRENNER..

HEY, MAN, I KNEW YOU'D COME THROUGH IT. I NEVER GAVE UP HOPE!

LISTEN, BRENNER, I'LL BE HOME BY TOMORROW. IF THAT HOUSE ISN'T EXACTLY THE WAY I LEFT IT, I'LL HAVE YOUR HIDE! YOU HEAR ME?

HEY, NOT TO WORRY, MAN, THE HOUSE IS FINE..

ACTUALLY, I'VE SORT OF IMPROVED IT.

DUKE zeke Brenner, Esq.

KEEP OUT!

WELCOME HOME, DUKE! RAH! RAH! WAY TO GO, DUKE! WHOOPIE!

WHAT'S GOING ON HERE? WHERE THE HELL'S THE BAND, BRENNER?

UH.. YOU DIDN'T TELL ME YOU WANTED A BAND, MAN.

THERE WAS SUPPOSED TO BE A BAND! AND WHERE'S THE PRESS? WHAT HAPPENED TO MY HERO'S WELCOME?

HEY, YOU'RE A HERO TO ME, DUKE! I EVEN GOT A GREEN RIBBON FOR YOU!

IT'S SUPPOSED TO BE YELLOW, PINHEAD.

OH. I COULDN'T REMEMBER. I'M NOT INTO TONY ORLANDO, MAN.

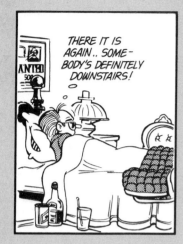

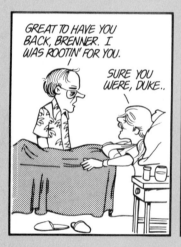

122

THE NURSE TELLS ME THEY'RE SPRINGING YOU TOMORROW, SPORT..

THAT'S RIGHT, LIEUTENANT. HOW'S YOUR MANHUNT GOING?

NOT SO GOOD, KID. YOU HAVE ANY IDEAS WHERE DUKE MIGHT BE?

WELL, MY GUESS IS HE'S JUST LAYING LOW, TAKING ODD JOBS UNTIL THE HEAT'S OFF.

KNOW ANY FRIENDS HE MIGHT TRY TO MAKE CONTACT WITH?

HMM.. NONE I CAN THINK OF, EXCEPT MAYBE THAT CRAZY CHINESE CHICK WHO USED TO WORK FOR HIM.

I CAME AS SOON AS I COULD, SIR.

HI, SANTA! I'D LIKE..

TAKE A HIKE, KID.

YOU WANTED TO SEE ME, SIR?

YEAH, HONEY, I'VE GOT A SURE-FIRE INVESTMENT I WANT TO DISCUSS WITH YOU.

BUT, SIR, I..

HEY, SANTA!

NOT NOW, KID.

SANTA, YOU'RE NOTHING BUT A BALD, SKINNY FAKE!

YEAH, WELL, YOU'RE NOTHING BUT A SNOTTY-FACED, WHIMPERING LITTLE GREEDHEAD!

YOU HAVE A NICE TOUCH, SIR.

THANKS. WHY DON'T WE GO SOMEPLACE QUIETER?

WAAH!

NOT THAT I HAVE ANY MONEY, SIR, BUT WHAT'S YOUR INVESTMENT?

IT'S RIGHT HERE, HONEY. THE OPPORTUNITY OF A LIFETIME!

WHY, IT'S.. IT'S JUST A BOAT!

IT'S NOT JUST A BOAT, HONEY! IT'S A 2000 H.P. CABIN CRUISER! COMPLETELY OUTFITTED FOR FISHING CHARTERS OUT OF MIAMI!

THE DECK LOOKS A LITTLE SMALL, SIR. HOW MANY CAN SHE ACCOMMODATE?

WELL, NOT TOO MANY PASSENGERS, BUT THE CARGO HOLD IS BIG ENOUGH TO TAKE 50 BALES EASY!

BALES, SIR?

I MEAN, FISH. LOTS OF ROOM FOR FISH.

ANY MESSAGES FOR ME WHILE I WAS GONE, HONEY?

YES, SIR! WE GOT OUR FIRST JOB!

WE DID?

YES, SIR. A GENTLEMAN BY THE NAME OF DIAZ WANTS YOU TO GO OUT TO SOME FREIGHTER TONIGHT AND PICK UP A SMALL PARCEL HE'S EXPECTING!

HOT DAMN! THIS IS IT, HONEY! WE ARE GOING TO CLEAN UP!

HE FIGURES IT WON'T TAKE MORE THAN A HALF HOUR, SO I QUOTED HIM A PRICE OF $35.

YOU WHAT?

AS AN INTRODUCTORY RATE. HE SEEMED VERY PLEASED!

$35? YOU GAVE HIM A QUOTE OF $35?

YOU JUST HAVE TO MEET SOME FREIGHTER, SIR. IT'S ONLY A SMALL JOB.

SMALL JOB? HONEY, WHAT WOULD YOU SAY IF I TOLD YOU THAT THAT SMALL JOB COULD HAVE BEEN WORTH $50,000!

WELL?

I'D SAY THAT WAS A LITTLE HIGH. WE'RE JUST STARTING OUT.

I CAN'T BELIEVE I'M RISKING MY TAIL FOR A LOUSY 35 BUCKS!

WE HAVE OUR REPUTATION TO THINK OF, SIR. WE CAN'T RENEGE ON OUR COMMITMENTS.

YOU MEAN, YOUR COMMITMENTS! WHAT'S THE NAME OF THAT FREIGHTER AGAIN?

THE "SAN PEDRO," SIR. IF I MAY ASK, SIR, YOU'RE NOT GOING OUT DRESSED LIKE THAT, ARE YOU?

WHAT'S WRONG WITH HOW I'M DRESSED? I'M ON A MISSION, FOR GOD'S SAKE!

YES, SIR, BUT IT'S OUR FIRST DELIVERY. IT'S IMPORTANT THAT YOU MAKE A VERY GOOD IMPRESSION!

I SEE. WHAT DID YOU HAVE IN MIND, HONEY?

WELL, I THOUGHT MAYBE A NICE BLAZER, SIR. LIKE THE GUYS AT FEDERAL EXPRESS.

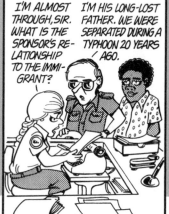

OKAY, AL, I NEED A DECKHAND, SO HERE'S THE DEAL. SINCE PER CAPITA INCOME IN HAITI IS ABOUT $300, I'M PREPARED TO DOUBLE THAT. YOU ALSO GET GRUB AND A BERTH ON THE BOAT.

NOW, IF YOU KEEP YOUR NOSE CLEAN, WE'LL GET ALONG FINE. BUT IF YOU SCREW UP EVEN **ONCE**, I'LL FEED YOU TO IMMIGRATION SO FAST IT'LL MAKE YOUR HEAD SPIN!

DON'T WORRY, ALPHONSE, IF HE TRIES THAT, YOU CAN ALWAYS TURN HIM IN TO THE POLICE. HE'S ON THE RUN JUST LIKE YOU!

OH?

HONEY!

JUST TRYING TO MAKE IT A FAIR FIGHT, SIR.

HEY, BOSS, COULD I HAVE A RAISE?

HEY, ALPHONSE, WHERE'S THE MAN?

HE'S OUT AT SEA, MR. ROD-RIGUEZ. HE LEFT THREE DAYS AGO.

WHEN'S HE DUE BACK? I GOT A JOB FOR HIM.

SORRY, SIR, MR. DUKE TOLD ME NOT TO AC-CEPT ANY NEW BUSI-NESS FOR HIM. HE'S GOING TO BE GONE AT LEAST FIVE WEEKS.

FIVE **WEEKS**? WHERE'S HE GOING, COLOMBIA?

NO, SIR, THE FALKLAND ISLANDS. HE'S TAKING A CHAR-TER OF SIGHTSEERS DOWN TO WATCH THE BRITISH BLOCKADE.

DON'T CRY FOR ME, AR-GENTINA!

HA! HA!

EXCUSE ME, SIR. WE'RE OUT OF ICE.

DAMN! WE HAVEN'T EVEN REACHED CUBA YET!

HAIL, **BRITANNIA**! BRITANNIA RULES THE WAVES! HA, HA!

THEY CER-TAINLY ARE A NOISY LOT, SIR.

OKAY BY ME, HONEY. THEY'RE PAYING PASSENGERS, TWO GRAND A HEAD! ALL WE GOTTA DO IS GET 'EM DOWN TO THE FALKLAND ISLANDS IN TIME FOR THE FIREWORKS.

I'LL TELL YOU, HONEY, THIS INVASION IS PURE GOLD! NOT TOO MANY WARS THESE DAYS WHERE YOU GET TWO WEEKS' NOTICE, YOU KNOW?

YES, SIR, IT WAS QUITE A BREAK.

FOR ONCE, WE HAD ENOUGH TIME TO GET A DECENT BROCHURE OUT.

I'M SURPRISED WE HAVEN'T SIGHTED ANY BRITISH SUPPLY VESSELS YET, HONEY. WE'RE RIGHT IN THE MIDDLE OF THE SOUTH ATLANTIC SHIPPING LANES..

WILL WE BE ARRIVING AT THE FALKLAND ISLANDS ON SCHEDULE, SIR?

I THINK SO. LET ME SEE.. OUR LAST RECORDED POSITION WAS HERE.. WE'RE BEARING SOUTHEAST AT 18 KNOTS.. HMM..

WELL, IT LOOKS GOOD. WE MAY POSSIBLY BE OFF BY AN INCH OR TWO, BUT IT'S NOTHING TO GET EXCITED ABOUT..

"ONE INCH EQUALS 1,000 MILES."

SO WE MISS THE OPENING FESTIVITIES. WHO'S GOING TO KNOW THE DIFFERENCE?

MAY I HAVE YOUR ATTENTION, PLEASE? THIS IS YOUR CAPTAIN SPEAKING..

THERE'S BEEN A LOT OF IRRESPONSIBLE TALK GOING AROUND TO THE EFFECT THAT WE'RE LOST. NOTHING COULD BE MORE MISLEADING. WE'RE SIMPLY A TAD OFF COURSE, UNDERSTANDABLE ON A 6,000-MILE VOYAGE.

WE'RE ALREADY THREE DAYS LATE!

WE'LL MISS THE INVASION!

IF YOU'LL CHECK YOUR CONTRACTS, YOU'LL SEE THAT ACTUAL HOSTILITIES WERE NOT GUARANTEED.

LIAR!

WE WANT OUR MONEY BACK!

BETTER TRAIN THAT DECK GUN DOWN HERE, HONEY.

THAT'S NOT GOING TO SOLVE ANYTHING, SIR.

I THINK I GOT THE PASSENGERS QUIETED DOWN, SIR. I GAVE THEM ALL DRINKS ON THE HOUSE.

WONDERFUL. THERE GOES OUR PROFIT MARGIN.

IT'S BETTER THAN A FULL-SCALE RIOT, SIR, AND.. HEY! LOOK OUT FOR THAT REEF!

REEF? WHERE?

CRUNCH!

SHUDDER!

WE WANT OUR MONEY BACK!

NOW YOU'VE DONE IT, SIR!

IT'S THESE DAMN OUTDATED CHARTS!

..AND WHILE I WAS TRYING TO QUELL THE MUTINY, WE HIT THIS DAMN REEF!

IT WASN'T HIS FAULT, THOUGH. THE CHART WAS NEARLY THREE YEARS OUT OF DATE.

AND WHO MIGHT YOU BE, YOUNG LADY?

I MIGHT BE HONEY, SIR. I WAS THE PURSER ON THE "RUSTY NAIL". NOW I'M MR. DUKE'S GAL FRIDAY.

REALLY? ARE YOU SURE YOU'D LIKE TO BE RESCUED, MR. DUKE? MOST MEN **DREAM** OF BEING SHIPWRECKED ON AN ISLAND WITH A CHARMING YOUNG LADY!

HELL, SO DO I, BUT HONEY AND I WERE THE ONLY SURVIVORS.

COMPLIMENT RECEIVED ON THIS END, SIR.

HARD TO BELIEVE, ISN'T IT, HONEY? DOWN TO OUR LAST WEEK'S RATION OF TEQUILA, AND WE'RE RESCUED BY A COUPLE OF BIRD-WATCHERS!

I WAS BEGINNING TO THINK WE WERE DONE FOR, WEREN'T YOU, HONEY?

NOT REALLY, SIR. I WAS PRETTY SURE WE'D MAKE IT.

OH, YEAH? HOW COME?

UM..WELL, ACTUALLY, I HAVE A SMALL CONFESSION, SIR. I SAW THE FERRY COME OVER HERE ABOUT A MONTH AGO.

SAY WHAT?

I JUST THOUGHT IT MORE IMPORTANT THAT WE HAVE SOME TIME TO OURSELVES.

HOW MUCH LONGER BEFORE THE FERRY GETS HERE, SIR?

IT SHOULD BE HERE MOMENTARILY. ANXIOUS TO BE LEAVING, ARE YOU?

ACTUALLY, SIR, I'M A LITTLE AMBIVALENT. DUKE AND I HAD SOME WONDERFUL TIMES HERE.

I GUESS I'M ALSO A LITTLE LET DOWN. WHEN WE FIRST ARRIVED, I CLAIMED THE ISLAND FOR CHINA. I THOUGHT I'D DISCOVERED A NEW VACATION SPOT FOR THE MASSES TO COME TO.

YOU CLAIMED MATAGORDA FOR **CHINA**?

WELL, MOST OF IT. I LOST THE MINERAL RIGHTS TO DUKE IN A POKER GAME.

WHAT DO YOU MEAN, IT FELL THROUGH, DUCKS?

THE STUDIO GOT COLD FEET. IT SEEMS EVERYONE IN TOWN IS DOING A DE LOREAN MOVIE. SID CAN'T GET ANY OF HIS CALLS RETURNED ANYMORE.

BUT AREN'T WE SCHEDULED TO START SHOOTING SOON?

DON'T WORRY, THIS PROJECT MEANS TOO MUCH TO ME TO GIVE UP NOW. I FIGURED OUT ANOTHER WAY TO RAISE THE MONEY.

YOU DID?

SURE. I JUST ASKED MYSELF, "WHAT WOULD JOHN DE LOREAN DO IN A SITUATION LIKE THIS?"

DUCKS.. NO!

RELAX, ALICE, IT'S PERFECTLY SAFE. I'M A PRO.

HEY, BABE, DO I HAVE TO PAINT YOU A PICTURE? THE PROJECT IS DEAD! THE MAJORS WON'T TOUCH IT!

SO WE'LL GO INDEPENDENT. I CAN RAISE THE CASH. ALL I NEED IS $50,000 DEVELOPMENT MONEY.

YOU'RE DREAMING, KID.

I SWEAR, SID, THAT'S ALL I NEED. IF I DON'T TURN IT INTO $10 MILLION BY NEXT MONDAY, I'LL PAY YOU BACK DOUBLE!

$10 MILLION BY NEXT MONDAY? HOW DO YOU PROPOSE TO DO THAT?

UH.. ON THE STOCK MARKET.

HEE, HEE! OKAY, I'LL BITE. I'LL HAVE MAGGIE DRAW UP A CHECK.

ACTUALLY, MAN, I NEED IT IN SMALL BILLS. JUST HAVE HER PUT IT IN A PAPER SACK.

YOU ROCCO?

MAYBE. WHO WANTS TO KNOW?

DUKE. LEO SENT ME. I UNDERSTAND YOU HAVE SOME MERCHANDISE TO SHOW ME.

YOU GOT THE MONEY?

WOULD I COME ALL THE WAY OUT HERE IF I DIDN'T?

OKAY, ROOM 101. CORAL MOTEL, ACROSS THE STREET. IN TEN MINUTES.

EXCUSE ME, WHAT'S HE SELLING? CAN I GET SOME, TOO?

ABORT.

SORRY. ONE-TIME OFFER.

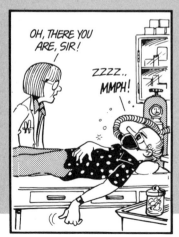

..AND CALL THE LABOR MINISTRY. WE'RE GOING TO NEED SCABS TO SERVE LUNCH AFTER THE CEREMONY.

THAT WON'T BE NECESSARY, SIR. I SETTLED THE KITCHEN WORKER STRIKE LAST NIGHT.

YOU DID? NOW, THAT'S THE BEST NEWS I'VE HAD ALL WEEK! GOOD WORK, HONEY!

THANK YOU, SIR. I WONDER IF YOU'D LIKE TO GO THROUGH THE LIST OF TODAY'S HONORARY DEGREE RECIPIENTS.

SURE, WHY NOT? LET'S SEE.. PAUL LUMIÈRE. JEANNE GENOT. PIERRE BERGER. ADRIENNE D'ARCY. IMPRESSIVE LINE-UP, HONEY!

YES, SIR.

WHO THE HELL ARE THEY?

THE KITCHEN STAFF.

ARE THE STUDENTS ALL LINED UP FOR THE ACADEMIC PROCESSION, DEAN HONEY?

AS MANY AS WE COULD FIND, YES, SIR.

AS MANY AS YOU COULD FIND?

WELL, SIR, THE HURRICANE LAST WEEK CAUSED SOME BIG SWELLS ON THE NORTH SHORE. A LOT OF THE STUDENTS ARE SURFING.

SURFING? THE MORNING OF MY INAUGURATION? DAMMIT, DEAN HONEY, I WILL **NOT** TOLERATE THIS KIND OF DISRESPECT TOWARD THE OFFICE OF THE PRESIDENCY!

I WANT THEM EXPELLED! EVERY LAST MOTHER'S SON!

YOU CAN'T DO THAT, SIR. YOU PUT THEIR TUITION INTO FIVE-YEAR BONDS.

BEFORE I INTRODUCE THE INAUGURAL SPEAKER, A FEW WORDS. IN THE MONTHS AHEAD, YOU WILL ALL STUDY MEDICINE. YOU WILL PLAY GOLF. YOU WILL LEARN ABOUT TAX SHELTERS. IN SHORT, YOU WILL BECOME DOCTORS!

BUT COME FEBRUARY, LADIES AND GENTLEMEN, YOU WILL DO THE **MOST IMPORTANT** THING YOU'LL EVER DO IN YOUR LIVES! YOU WILL MEET ST. GEORGE'S IN GRENADA, AND YOU WILL **DESTROY THEM** IN **VOLLEYBALL!**

YEAAA!

CLAP! CLAP! CLAP! CLAP!

GRENADA SUCKS EGGS! GRENADA SUCKS EGGS!

POINT SPREAD CITY!

THEY SURE HAVE A LOT OF SCHOOL SPIRIT, SIR.

BOY, IT'S GREAT TO SEE YOU AGAIN, UNCLE DUKE. IT'S BEEN MUCH TOO LONG!

SURE HAS. GOT THE CERTIFIED CHECK FOR YOUR TUITION?

YUP. HERE YOU GO. I HOPE THIS WORKS OUT. DAD HAD TO TAKE OUT A PRETTY STIFF LOAN..

HE WON'T REGRET IT, BOY. HE'LL BE WATCHING YOU GRADUATE IN THREE SHORT YEARS! FOUR YEARS, MAX.

I DUNNO, UNCLE DUKE. I'VE NEVER EVEN TAKEN BIO BEFORE.

NEITHER HAVE A LOT OF OUR STUDENTS. DEAN HONEY HERE IS TUTORING HALF THE VOLLEYBALL TEAM!

VOLLEYBALL? THERE'S TIME FOR VOLLEYBALL?

MOST OF THE GAMES ARE FIXED, BUT IT'S STILL GOOD FUN.

WELCOME TO CLUB PRE-MED, SIR!

TO THE MEDICAL COLLEGE! ON THE DOUBLE!

OUI, MONSIEUR!

WHAT A QUAINT WAY TO GET AROUND!

NICE, HUH?

IF THERE'S ONE THING I LOVE, IT'S A GOOD SERVICE ECONOMY. THEY DON'T ALWAYS DO IT WELL HERE, BUT THEY DO IT FOR NEXT TO NOTHING!

I DIDN'T EVEN KNOW THEY HAD RICKSHAWS IN HAITI.

THEY DON'T. I HAD IT SHIPPED IN. YO, HONEY! YOU STILL WITH US?

YES, SIR! PANT! PANT!

..AND IN ADDITION TO BEING FULLY EQUIPPED, ALL OUR LABS HAVE SHAG CARPETING!

THIS IS INCREDIBLE!

I HAD NO IDEA THAT BABY DOC WAS SO OPULENTLY APPOINTED! I EXPECTED PALM FROND ROOFS AND CANVAS TENTS!

THIS PLACE HAS ALL THE OLD WORLD CHARM OF A TROPICAL OXFORD. ONE CAN ALMOST SEE THE DONS SIPPING PORT ON THE VERANDA!

ACTUALLY, THREE MONTHS AGO, IT WAS A BROTHEL.

I MEAN, HOW MANY CLASSROOMS STILL HAVE RED VELVET WALLPAPER?

AND THEN WHAT?

WELL, ONCE I BOUGHT THE BROTHEL, I GOT THE LOCAL AUTHORITIES TO RAZE MOST OF THE SURROUNDING SHANTIES.

AFTER THAT, IT WAS JUST A MATTER OF PUTTING IN THE TENNIS COURTS AND SENDING OUT BROCHURES. THE REST IS OFF-SHORE EDUCATION / HISTORY!

IT'S AN AMAZING STORY, UNCLE DUKE, SIMPLY AMAZING!

THANKS. WELL, I BETTER GET BACK TO THE O.R. I WAS IN THE MIDDLE OF SURGERY WHEN YOU CALLED.

SURGERY? BUT.. BUT YOU'RE NOT A DOCTOR.

I KNOW, BUT IT'S AN EMERGENCY. AND OUR REGULAR CUTTER IS OUT SNORKELING.

CURTIS, THIS IS YOUR NEW ROOMMATE! SAY HELLO TO.. UH.. JOE SMITH!

HI, JOE! WELCOME TO BABY DOC.. HEY, DID ANYONE EVER TELL YOU YOU LOOK LIKE ZONKER HARRIS?

YEAH. I GET THAT ALL THE TIME.

WAIT A MINUTE! YOU **ARE** ZONKER HARRIS! I SAW YOU TAN AGAINST GEORGE HAMILTON IN THE '81 SUN SPRINTS! I GREW UP ON YOU, MAN! I CAN'T BELIEVE YOU'RE **HERE!**

OH, MY GOD. AND THE ROOM'S A MESS!

SORRY, SIR. I TRIED.

NO PROBLEM. I CAN HANDLE IT.

GOOD LORD, CURTIS. YOU ACTUALLY **OWN** A ZONKER HARRIS SIGNATURE MODEL TANNING REFLECTOR?

YES, SIR, MR. HARRIS!

HEY, HEY, WHAT'S THIS "MR. HARRIS" STUFF, CURTIS? WE'RE ROOMIES, FOR GOD'S SAKE!

YES, SIR. COULD YOU SIGN THIS, PLEASE? IT'S NOT FOR ME. IT'S FOR.. UH.. MY AUNT.

GLAD TO. WHAT'S YOUR AUNT'S NAME?

HER NAME? UH.. CURTIS. AUNT CURTIS. I WAS NAMED AFTER HER. REALLY.

IF YOU SAY SO.

GOD, THIS IS SO UNCOOL! WHAT AM I **DOING?**

161

YOU GOT BACK JUST IN TIME, HONEY. I'M GOING TO NEED YOUR HELP DURING THE MEDICAL CONFERENCE WE'RE HOSTING THIS WEEK.

THE COLLEGE IS HOSTING A MEDICAL CONFERENCE, SIR?

YEAH, ON ECSTASY. THE D.E.A., IN ITS WISDOM, HAS JUST DECLARED ECSTASY A BIG, BAD, SCHEDULE I NO-NO!

I DON'T THINK I'M FAMILIAR WITH THAT DRUG, SIR.

SHRINKS HAVE BEEN USING IT FOR YEARS, BUT THE KIDS, AS USUAL, RUINED IT FOR EVERYONE. THEY TURNED MDMA INTO A DAMN PARTY DRUG!

MDMA? OH, YOU MEAN METHYLENEDIOXYMETHAMPHETAMINE!

KNOCK IT OFF, HONEY.

YOU SEE, HONEY, ECSTASY IS A VERY PROMISING PSYCHOTHERAPEUTIC TOOL. BUT THANKS TO THE FEDS, THE WORK OF TOP MDMA RESEARCHERS HAS BEEN NIPPED IN THE BUD!

WHAT I'LL BE PROPOSING AT THE CONFERENCE IS THAT SOME OF THESE PEOPLE JOIN OUR FACULTY AND CONTINUE THEIR IMPORTANT WORK RIGHT HERE!

I SEE.

SIR, I HOPE THIS ISN'T JUST A FRONT FOR...

EVERY PENNY WILL GO TO SCHOLARSHIPS, HONEY.

SO WHAT'S THE HOLD-UP, DEAN HONEY?

THE STEWARDESS SAYS THEY WON'T GET OFF THE PLANE, SIR. THEY CLAIM THEY'RE HAPPY WHERE THEY ARE.

DAMN! I KNEW THIS WOULD HAPPEN!

WHENEVER YOU PUT A BUNCH OF HOT-SHOT DRUG DESIGNERS TOGETHER, THE FIRST THING THEY DO IS SWAP COMPOUNDS!

ANYONE HERE WANT TO HELP ME PROMOTE GOOD?

I DO! LET ME GET MY THINGS! IS THIS HOME OR ABROAD?

WITH THAT SIMPLE CHEMICAL RECONFIGURATION, "INTENSITY" CAME KICKING INTO THE WORLD.

WE JUST FIGURED WHY GO WITH TWO OXYGEN MOLECULES WHEN ONE WILL DO?

THE DRUG, BY THE WAY, IS INSANELY GREAT. WE FORESEE MYRIAD APPLICATIONS IN PSYCHIATRY AND PROFESSIONAL FOOTBALL.

ANY SIDE EFFECTS, DR. GORP?

YES, BUT INTRIGUING ONES. FOR EXAMPLE, "INTENSITY" GIVES THE ILLUSION OF SUBSTANCE TO YOUR ALTER EGO.

UH..HOLD IT, ALBIE. ARE YOU IMPLYING I'M ONLY A SIDE EFFECT?

IT'S ONLY TEMPORARY, THOUGH.

©B Trudeau

DR. GORP, ARE THERE ANY OTHER SIDE EFFECTS ASSOCIATED WITH "INTENSITY" WE SHOULD BE AWARE OF?

WELL, YES, "INTENSITY" SEEMS TO SHARE SOME OF THE MILD UNPLEASANTNESS ATTRIBUTED TO ITS CHEMICAL COUSINS..

..LIKE NAUSEA, TIGHTENING OF THE JAW, SOME DIZZINESS..

BAD NEWS, ALBIE. TRICKY DICK GOT THE G.O.P. NOMINATION!

..AND, OF COURSE, FLASHBACKS.

DR. GORP, HAVE YOU WORKED OUT THE ETHICAL RAMIFICATIONS OF MARKETING A DESIGNER DRUG AS UNTESTED AS "INTENSITY"?

NO, BUT MY TWIN BROTHER BUNNY HAS, RIGHT, BUNNY?

THAT'S RIGHT, ALBIE..

I'VE DONE A LOT OF RESEARCH ON THE MATTER, AND I CAN ASSURE YOU, MORALS-WISE, WE'RE ON TERRA FIRMA.

SIR, IF YOU HIRE THE SIDE EFFECT, I'M QUITTING.

NOW, DEAN HONEY, I CAN'T BREAK UP THE ACT.

©B Trudeau

DEAN HONEY, NOT A **WORD** OF MY WINDFALL TO ANYONE UNTIL I THINK THIS THROUGH, OKAY?

NOT EVEN YOUR UNCLE DUKE, SIR?

ESPECIALLY MY UNCLE DUKE! IT'S A SECRET, UNDERSTAND? A SECRET!

A SECRET. YES, SIR. YOU CAN COUNT ON ME.

$23 MILLION! I MUST BE DREAMING..

IT'S SORT OF A SECRET, SIR.

YOU WERE RIGHT TO BRING THIS TO ME, HONEY.

ZONK! HOW'S IT GOING, STRANGER? LONG TIME!

I SAW YOU THIS MORNING AT BREAKFAST, UNCLE DUKE.

THAT WAS YOU? YOU LOOK DIFFERENT! DONE SOMETHING WITH YOUR HAIR?

WHAT DO YOU WANT, UNCLE DUKE?

WELL, I'VE SOME BAD NEWS, SON. THE NEW HEATING OIL BILL CAME IN. I'M GOING TO HAVE TO RAISE ROOM AND BOARD TO $1,000 A DAY.

WHAT?

STRICTLY ON AN ABILITY-TO-PAY BASIS, OF COURSE.

I'LL KILL HER.

HE USED HIS LOVER'S WILES ON ME, SIR.

WELL, BOY, YOUR LIFE'S COURSE HAS TAKEN A DANGEROUS, HAIRPIN TURN. LIKE IT OR NOT, YOU NOW HAVE TO ANSWER TO AN AWESOME NEW MASTER—MONEY!

NO WAY, UNCLE DUKE. MONEY DOESN'T CHANGE A THING. I'M CONTINUING TO STUDY TO BE A DOCTOR!

NEPHEW, THINK FOR A MOMENT. WHY IS IT YOU WANTED TO **BE** A DOCTOR?

WELL, TO MAKE..

GOOD POINT.

ZONKER, DON'T BE AFRAID TO ASK FOR HELP IN THE DAYS AHEAD.

THAT'LL HAVE TO BE THE LAST QUESTION, BOYS! I HAVE TO GET BACK AND HIT THE BOOKS!

SO SAID LOTTERY WINNER ZONKER HARRIS THIS MORNING AS HE RETURNED TO CLASSES HERE AT THE ACADEMICALLY GRUELING BABY DOC COLLEGE OF PHYSICIANS.

$23 MILLION JUST DOESN'T SEEM TO HAVE CHANGED THIS UNAFFECTED YOUNG MAN AND HIS BOYHOOD DREAM OF BECOMING A DOCTOR.

YO, BABE! I'LL GIVE YOU TEN GRAND TO TAKE MY BIO-CHEM EXAM!

OKAY.

I GOT THE RICKSHAW ALL WARMED UP TO TAKE YOU TO THE AIRPORT, LAD!

UNCLE DUKE, I DON'T WANT A RICKSHAW.

THEN I'LL HAVE THE LIMO SENT ROUND. LET ME GIVE YOU A HAND HERE.

YOU CERTAINLY ARE BEING CONSIDERATE, UNCLE DUKE.

THANKS, NEPHEW.

A TEENY BIT OUT OF CHARACTER, WOULDN'T YOU SAY?

YOU'RE RIGHT. WANT ME TO SEE A SHRINK? I WILL IF YOU'RE WORRIED.

HAVE A GREAT CHRISTMAS HOLIDAY, NEPHEW. HERE'S A LITTLE SOMETHING TO SLIP UNDER THE OL' TREE!

I.. I DON'T KNOW WHAT TO SAY, UNCLE DUKE.

IT'S A BABY DOC SCHOOL TIE. SO YOU WON'T FORGET ABOUT US, GUY!

UNCLE DUKE, DO I DETECT A NEW NOTE OF OBSEQUIOUSNESS FROM YOU SINCE THE LOTTERY, OR IS IT JUST MY IMAGINATION?

YES.

YES WHAT?

YES, SIR.

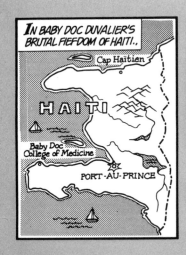

THE INTERVIEW'S ON? FANTASTIC!

ANY GROUND RULES? WHAT'S HE PREPARED TO COVER?

UH-HUH.. RETIREMENT, RIGHT.. HIS PLACE IN HISTORY.. UH-HUH.. NO, I DON'T HAVE ANY PROBLEMS WITH THAT.

TIP O'NEILL?

BABY DOC.

LOOK AT THOSE FACES. ARROGANT TO THE END! WOULDN'T YOU **LOVE** TO KNOW WHAT THE DUVALIERS SPIRITED OUT WITH THEM THE NIGHT THEY FLED?

WELL, YES AND NO..

FRIDAY, FEB

Duvalier Lea

The final drive to the airport. AP

"powerful as a monkey's tail." U.S. of-
decided to give up his auth—
Baby Doc has l..

SOMETIMES, THE REAL STORY CAN BE..

..UNSPEAKABLY HIDEOUS!

..AND RICK'S ALREADY LEFT TO VISIT HIM IN EXILE. IT'S ONE OF THE FEW INTERVIEWS DUVALIER'S EVER GIVEN!

GOODNESS! THAT **IS** A REMARKABLE ASSIGNMENT!

IT SHOULD YIELD SOME ABSOLUTELY **FASCINATING** INSIGHTS INTO THE GENESIS OF EVIL!

..AND THEN THE OTHER KIDS STARTED CALLING ME "BASKETHEAD."

SO THAT'S WHEN YOU DECIDED TO GET EVEN?

MR. EX-PRESIDENT-FOR-LIFE, ALMOST EVERYONE WAS SHOCKED BY HOW QUICKLY YOUR REGIME SEEMED TO COLLAPSE..

WERE YOU YOUR-SELF SURPRISED AT HOW FAST THINGS CAME UNRAVELLED?

NOT AT ALL. I KNEW THERE WERE SUBVERSIVES IN HAITI.

JUST LAST JULY, WE HAD A DEMOCRATIC REFERENDUM ON MY RULE. THE VOTE FOR ME WAS 4,500,000 TO 2.

SO YOU HAD AN INKLING..

ALL IT TAKES IS A COUPLE OF BAD APPLES.

MR. DUVALIER, DO YOU THINK YOUR WIFE'S ILL-TIMED EXTRAVAGANCES CONTRIBUTED TO YOUR FINAL DOWNFALL?

HOW DO YOU MEAN?

WELL, FOR INSTANCE, HER LEAVING FOR A $1.7 MILLION SHOPPING SPREE IN PARIS WHILE HAITI WAS IN THE MIDST OF A SEVERE ECONOMIC CRISIS.

$1.7 MILLION? SHE SPENT $1.7 MILLION IN PARIS?

REPORT-EDLY.

WHAT'D SHE DO WITH THE REST OF IT!

UM.. I DON'T KNOW. I'D RATHER NOT GET CAUGHT IN THE MIDDLE HERE.

I'M AFRAID YOU'LL HAVE TO EXCUSE ME NOW, MR. RED-FERN. I HAVE AN-OTHER ENGAGE-MENT.

OF COURSE, MR. DUVAL-IER.

I'LL HAVE MY MAN DRIVE YOU TO THE AIRPORT.

THAT'S OKAY. I DON'T WANT TO TROUBLE ANYONE..

NO TROUBLE AT ALL! LÉGUME!

"LÉGUME"?

YOU BELLOWED, YOUR PARIAH-SHIP?

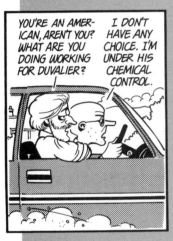

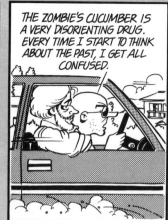

MR. DUPUIS? YES, THIS IS MR. HARRIS. I UNDERSTAND YOU REPRESENT EX-PRESIDENT-FOR-LIFE DUVALIER.

GOOD, GOOD. I'LL TELL YOU WHY I CALLED. I'M VERY INTERESTED IN ACQUIRING ONE OF HIS ZOMBIE SLAVES, A MR. LÉGUME.

WHY? SENTIMENTAL REASONS, MOSTLY. MAY WE NEGOTIATE? GREAT. I'M GOING TO PUT ON MY HIGH-POWERED LEGAL COUNSEL, MS. JOANIE "JAWS" CAUCUS.

"JAWS" HERE.

RING! RING! HEY, **JAWS!** THE ATTORNEY GENERAL ON LINE **TWO!**

HOW FAR DO YOU WANT TO GO WITH THIS?

AS FAR AS WE HAVE TO. I'M A RICH MAN.

MR. DUPUIS? SINCE THE PURCHASE OF HUMAN BEINGS IS FORBIDDEN OUTSIDE OF PRO SPORTS, MY CLIENT HAS ADVISED ME TO OFFER YOU A "FINDER'S FEE" FOR MR. DUKE'S RETURN.

WHAT DO WE HAVE IN MIND? WELL, THAT'S DIFFICULT TO SAY, MR. DUPUIS. HOW CAN WE MEASURE THE VALUE OF A PERSON? IS IT POSSIBLE TO SET A PRICE FOR A HUMAN LIFE?

$10 MILLION. TAKE IT OR LEAVE IT.

PASS. WE'RE NOT TALKING MOTHER TERESA HERE.

EXCUSE ME, SIR. THERE'S A RUMOR IN THE SLAVE QUARTERS THAT I'M ON THE BLOCK.

THAT'S RIGHT, LÉGUME. A RICH AMERICAN WANTS TO BUY YOU. HE CLAIMS TO BE YOUR NEPHEW.

NEPHEW? YOU MEAN, **ZONKER?** OH, PLEASE, YOUR MALIGNANCY, NOT **HIM!** ZONKER'S A **MONSTER!** CRUELTY INCARNATE! HE'S **EVIL ON THE HOOF!**

OR IS THAT MY COUSIN ALFREDO? I GET THEM MIXED UP..

IT DOESN'T MATTER. THE DEAL IS AS GOOD AS DONE!

COULDN'T YOU SELL HIM ONE OF THE OTHER GUYS?

SORRY. I ALREADY SENT HIM YOUR BROCHURE.

.. AND THOSE ARE DUKE'S HEALTH CERTIFICATES. I HAD THEM POUCHED OVER FROM FRANCE.

GOOD THINKING, JOANIE.

LET'S SEE HERE.. HIS WEIGHT IS 145.. THAT'S ABOUT RIGHT. BLOOD PRESSURE IS 20 OVER 30.. GOOD, GOOD..

20 OVER 30 IS GOOD?

IT'S NORMAL FOR A ZOMBIE. THEY'RE PRETTY MELLOW. AHA! HIS DENTAL X-RAY! YUP, IT'S DUKE, ALL RIGHT!

HOW CAN YOU TELL?

HIS MOLARS. THAT'S OLD MICRO-FILM FROM HIS SMUGGLING DAYS.

$4.5 MILLION? THAT DOESN'T WORK FOR US. HOW ABOUT 4.2 ON A 15-YEAR SCHEDULE WITH COLAS? WHAT? NO.. THAT WON'T DO..

WE'RE WASTING VALUABLE TIME HERE, COUNSELOR. LET ME GIVE IT A SHOT..

UM.. MR. DUPUIS, MY CLIENT WOULD LIKE TO TALK TO YOU PERSONALLY..

DUPUIS? HARRIS HERE! THIS ISN'T AN ARAB BAZAAR, MON AMI! ALL I'VE GOT IS $17 MIL CASH! TAKE IT OR LEAVE IT!

DONE. SEE, YOU JUST HAVE TO BE FORCEFUL.

OH, ZONKER..

IT WAS 3:45 A.M. WHEN THE NIGHT PORTER SIGNED FOR THE CRATE FROM MARSEILLES...

SAR? SAR?

HUNKLE DOOOKE?

SIR? CAN YOU HEAR ME?

HE DOESN'T LOOK SO GOOD...

181

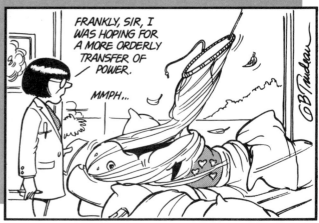

WHAT'S THE WORD FROM THE FRONT, DON?

IT'S CATCHING ON, SIR. CANDIDATES ALL OVER THE COUNTRY ARE ENLISTING IN YOUR WAR AGAINST DRUGS!

UNFORTUNATELY, AS A CAMPAIGN ISSUE, IT SEEMS TO HAVE ONE DRAWBACK: EVERYONE'S ON THE SAME SIDE OF THE ISSUE.

IF ONLY WE COULD FIND A STRAW MAN, SOME HIGH-PROFILE LIBERTARIAN CRAZY OR STUPID ENOUGH TO TAKE A STAND FOR DRUG ABUSE!

I'M NEEDED, HONEY.

SIR! YOU SAID SOMETHING!

...AND THE FOLLOWING PARTS OF THE BILL OF RIGHTS HAVE BEEN SUSPENDED...

SOME WAR ON DRUGS! IT'S SCORCHED EARTH TIME! I'VE GOT TO GET HOME, PRONTO!

THEY'LL LISTEN TO ME! I'M PRESIDENT OF A RESPECTED MEDICAL COLLEGE!

UH...YOU WERE, SIR. LAST WEEK, JUDGE DUPUIS RULED YOU INCOMPETENT.

DUPUIS? THAT TREACHEROUS OLD CROCK OF SLIME! I'VE HAD HIM ON RETAINER FOR TWO YEARS! YOU CAN'T TRUST ANYONE THESE DAYS!

LISTEN, HONEY...

PRESIDENT HONEY.

HELP ME FIND MY SNEAKERS, HONEY! MY COUNTRY NEEDS ME!

IT'S TOO LATE, SIR. EVERYTHING HAS CHANGED SINCE YOU'VE BEEN GONE.

GONE? I DIDN'T GO ANYWHERE! DID I?

PEOPLE ARE NO LONGER TOLERANT OF DRUG USE. THE COST HAS BEEN TOO HIGH. A LOT OF US NOW THINK IT WAS WRONG TO LOOK THE OTHER WAY!

AFTER NANCY REAGAN'S SPEECH, I REALIZED THAT I'D BEEN REMISS, THAT BY STANDING IDLY DURING YOUR SELF-DESTRUCTIVE BINGES, I'D LET YOU DOWN AS A FRIEND.

YEAH, WELL, DON'T LOSE ANY SLEEP OVER...

I'VE TURNED YOU IN, SIR.

HEY, DID YOU GUYS KNOW THE HOUSE WAS SURROUNDED?

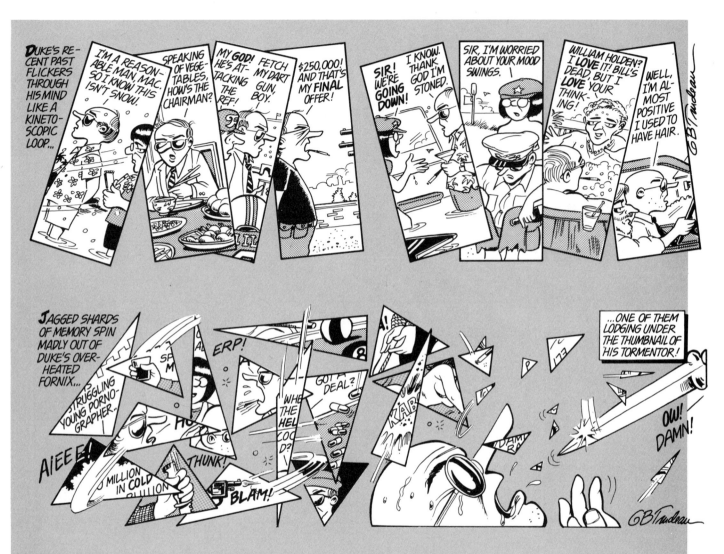

HI. I'M SAL DOONESBURY, AND I'D LIKE TO WELCOME YOU TO THE INSTITUTE FOR IMMACULATE CONTRACEPTION, POPULARLY KNOWN AS WHOOPEE U.!

AS DISTRICT SALES MANAGER TRAINEES, YOU ARE HERE TO LEARN THE WHOOPEE WAY OF LIFE. IT MAY BE THE MOST IMPORTANT COURSE OF INSTRUCTION YOU EVER TAKE!

WHEN YOU SELL DR. WHOOPEE, YOU ARE SELLING HOPE. YOU BECOME PART OF THE SOLUTION. YOU'LL BE SAYING NO TO A MYRIAD OF SOCIAL PROBLEMS!

OF COURSE, YOU'LL ALSO BE WINNING FABULOUS PRIZES!

SAL, HOW MANY POINTS FOR THE CATCHER'S MITT?

BEFORE WE START, LET'S TAKE A LOOK AT THIS MOTIVATIONAL VIDEO MESSAGE FROM DR. WHOOPEE'S FOUNDER AND CHAIRMAN!

CLIK!

YOU KNOW, WHEN I FOUNDED DR. WHOOPEE LAST YEAR, I SWORE MY PRODUCTS WOULD BE THE FINEST AVAILABLE ON THE MARKET! WELL, I DELIVERED ON THAT PLEDGE.

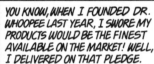

HOW DO YOU KNOW? HOW DO YOU KNOW OUR LINE IS ALL I SAY IT IS? HOW DO YOU KNOW WE USE ONLY THE FINEST MATERIALS CURRENTLY AVAILABLE ANYWHERE IN THE CARIBBEAN BASIN?

TRUST ME.

AN INSPIRATIONAL VIDEO FOR DR. WHOOPEE TRAINEES...

AS FOUNDER OF DR. WHOOPEE, I KEEP AN EAGLE EYE ON OUR PRODUCT FROM START TO FINISH!

"DR. WHOOPEES ARE STILL MADE BY HAND BY LOCAL HAITIAN CRAFTSPEOPLE USING THE SAME TIME-HONORED METHODS I DEVELOPED BACK IN 1986."

"BY CONTRAST, OUR DISTRIBUTION IS STATE-OF-THE-ART. ORDERS ARE RELAYED BY SATELLITE AND PROCESSED BY COMPUTER!"

MEANWHILE, IN RESEARCH AND DEVELOPMENT...

EUREKA! PLAID!

DOONESBURY! WHY THE HELL HAVEN'T YOU MOVED THAT LAST CONSIGNMENT OF DR. WHOOPEES?

SORRY, SIR...

...BUT TWO OF MY TOP GUYS TOOK OFF FOR THE HARMONIC CONVERGENCE.

WHAT?

LISTEN, SAL, NO MORE HIPPIE HOLIDAYS! IF YOUR PEOPLE WANT TO CAVORT WITH SPOOKS, LET THEM DO IT ON THEIR OWN TIME! GOT IT?

EXCUSE ME, SIR, THERE'S A WILLIAM CASEY HERE TO SEE YOU.

UH...LET ME GET BACK TO YOU, SAL...

BILL...BILL CASEY... MY GOD, IT IS YOU!

LONG TIME, DUKE.

THIS IS ABSOLUTELY INCREDIBLE...

I MEAN, YOUR BEING HERE IN HAITI! AND LOOKING SO WELL! I MEAN, CONSIDERING THAT, YOU KNOW... I MEAN, THIS IS HARD TO... / TO...

LET'S CUT THE CRAP, BILL. YOU'RE DEAD.

A LEADING THEORY, IT'S TRUE.

HOW...HOW'D YOU PULL IT OFF, BILL? THE WHOLE WORLD THINKS YOU'RE DEAD!

I'M A SPOOK, DUKE. DECEIT HAS BEEN MY LIFE.

BUT... WHY?

TO PROTECT THE COVERT OPERATIONS SLUSH FUND, THE MISSING MILLIONS. I KNEW IT WOULD COME OUT IN THE HEARINGS, AND I DIDN'T WANT TO BE AROUND TO ANSWER ANY QUESTIONS!

IT'S TOO BRILLIANT A PLAN TO GIVE UP, DUKE. SINCE THE MONEY ISN'T APPROPRIATED, THE PRESIDENT WOULD HAVE A COMPLETELY DISCRETIONARY, ALBEIT ILLEGAL, COVERT CAPABILITY!

SO WHERE DO I FIT IN?

AS I SAY, IT'S ILLEGAL.

THE POSSIBILITIES ARE FANTASTIC, DUKE! WE COULD FUND THE CONTRAS, BUY THE AFGHANS NUKES, TERMINATE PANAMA'S PRESIDENT!

EXCUSE ME A MINUTE, WILL YOU, BILL?

HONEY!

YES, SIR?

AM I ON ANYTHING RIGHT NOW?

LET ME CHECK YOUR BOOK, SIR...

DUKE, LET ME COME RIGHT TO THE POINT...

I'M ALL EARS, BILL!

THIS COVERT ACTION SLUSH FUND IS THE GREATEST INNOVATION IN U.S. INTELLIGENCE IN A GENERATION. I'M PROUD OF IT. I DON'T WANT TO SEE IT DIE WITH ME!

NOR I, BILL.

I NEED YOUR HELP, DUKE. I NEED SOMEONE WHO CAN LEAD THE ILLEGAL COVERT OPERATIONS OF THIS COUNTRY INTO THE TWENTY-FIRST CENTURY!

GEE, I DUNNO, BILL. I GOT A LOT ON MY PLATE AND...

CLIK!

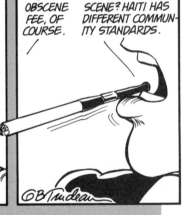

FOR AN OBSCENE FEE, OF COURSE.

OBSCENE? HOW OBSCENE? HAITI HAS DIFFERENT COMMUNITY STANDARDS.

OBVIOUSLY, DUKE, I CAN'T USE COMPANY PERSONNEL ANYMORE. THAT'S WHY I NEED YOU TO ASSEMBLE A COVERT ACTION TEAM!

HERE'S THE COMPLETE FINANCIAL RECORD. TAKE A LOOK, SO YOU KNOW WHAT YOU'VE GOT TO WORK WITH. I'LL GIVE YOU THE ACCOUNT NUMBER WHEN YOU'RE READY TO GO!

THERE'S NO TIME TO WASTE, DUKE. I'M NOT A WELL MAN. IN FACT...>COUGH!< I MAY NOT...

TOP SECRET

>COUGH!< >COUGH!< HACK! HACK!

CRASH!!

JEEZ, BILL, THIS IS ONE HELLUVA HAND-OFF.

190

...AND I PUT DOWN A HEAVY DEPOSIT ON 2 C-14s. AS FOR PERSONNEL, I'VE RETAINED NEARLY 40 CONTRACT PLAYERS, MOSTLY GERMAN MERCS. OKAY, BILL? ≈ WHEEZE! ≤

GOOD. SO ALL I NEED NOW IS YOUR SIGNATURE AND BANK ACCOUNT NUMBER. YOU **DO** RECALL THE NUMBER, DON'T YOU, BILL?

BILL?

LOOK, BILL, I'M OUT-OF-POCKET OVER 200 G'S HERE, SO I'D APPRECIATE... CROAK.

NO! NO **WAY!** I WILL **NOT** BE CHEATED! YOU WILL **NOT** DIE, CASEY!

WHAT **IS** THIS? ONE SECOND, I HAVE **MILLIONS** IN MY GRASP, THE NEXT, ALL I'VE GOT IS A DEAD C.I.A. DIRECTOR IN MY **BED!**

GET ME THE "NATIONAL ENQUIRER."

..AND FOR 50 GRAND, IT'S A **BARGAIN!** WHAT EXACTLY ARE YOU OFFERING THE "ENQUIRER," MR. DUKE?

ALL THE COLOR PIX YOU WANT, PLUS MY EXCLUSIVE STORY! AND YOU'RE SURE YOU HAVE THE BODY?

OF **COURSE** I HAVE THE BODY! I JUST SENT MY ASSISTANT OVER TO MY BUNGALOW TO PACK IT IN ICE!

EXCUSE ME, SIR, WHAT BODY? SHALL WE SAY ALL THE MONEY UP FRONT?

I'M A MAN OF RESPECT. I EXPECT TO BE TREATED LIKE ONE. YOU FOLLOW ME?

WHEN I SPOT SOMEONE $230,000, I EXPECT TO SEE IT AGAIN. I'M A BUSINESSMAN. IF I GET STIFFED, I LOSE FACE. AND THAT'S BAD FOR BUSINESS.

HEY, YOU WANT A NEW SUIT? YOU WANT I SHOULD HAVE YOU MEASURED FOR A SUIT, TOO?

UH... SURE. WOOL?

CONCRETE. YOU'RE IN A WORLD OF TROUBLE, DOG MEAT.

LOOK, I WAS **GOING** TO PAY YOU BACK! I **SWEAR** IT! BUT WHAT COULD I DO? WHO KNEW MY MOTHER WOULD NEED SURGERY?

PSST, SIR! DON'T YOU THINK YOU SHOULD LEVEL WITH THIS GUY? HE COULD BE A FEDERAL AGENT!

SHUT UP, HONEY. HE'S JOHN GOTTI, HEAD OF THE GAMBINO FAMILY!

OH.

CARRY ON, SIR.

YOU'VE GOT A MOTHER, RIGHT, BIG GUY? RIGHT?

LEMME TELL YOU SOMETHING, DUKE. I'M AN ACQUITTED MAN. I LIKE THE ACQUITTED LIFE VERY MUCH. I'M THE ROSE OF HOWARD BEACH!

SO I GOTTA BE CAREFUL, UNDERSTAND? THAT'S WHY I'M GONNA LET YOU GUESS WHAT I WANT FROM YOU, AND WHAT'LL HAPPEN TO YOU IF I DON'T GET IT.

YOU WANT 10% OF MY BUSINESS OR I GET MY HANDS BROKEN?

GUESS AGAIN.

YOU GET 90% OR I GET STUFFED INTO A CAR COMPACTER?

IS THAT A **GUESS**? HOW COME YOUSE GUYS DON'T GUESS THAT GOOD?

HEY, C'MON, BOSS, HE GOT LUCKY!

LOOK AT THE QUALITY! CHAMOIS LEATHER WALLS! BIRD'S EYE MAPLE TRIM! HAND-CARVED ONYX BATHROOMS! WE'RE TALKING **QUALITY!** A LEVEL OF QUALITY THAT'S HARD TO EXPLAIN!

LOOK HERE, **MORE** QUALITY...

EXCUSE ME, SIR. BY "QUALITY", YOU MEAN IT **COSTS** AN OBSCENE AMOUNT, RIGHT?

UH... RIGHT.

THERE ARE OTHER DEFINITIONS?

NONE THAT MATTER. I WAS JUST CHECKING.

LOOK AT THE PERFORMANCE QUALITY OF THIS BOAT! 17.5 KNOTS CRUISING SPEED! 8,500 MILES WITHOUT REFUELING! YOU CAN'T JUST **BUY** THIS KIND OF QUALITY, YOU HAVE TO **WILL** IT!

DO YOU THINK YOU CAN HANDLE HER, CAPTAIN?

NO PROBLEM, MR. TRUMP!

OKAY, SEE THAT LITTLE OUTBOARD OVER THERE?

WITH THE KIDS? YEAH, I SEE IT.

SWAMP IT.

PIECE OF CAKE.

ON THE BOARDWALK.

MAGNIFICENT, ISN'T SHE?

YEAH. IF YOU'RE A LITTLE BOY INTO GIGANTIC TOYS.

TAKES YOUR BREATH AWAY, DOESN'T IT?

I'LL SAY. YOU DON'T OFTEN SEE VULGARITY ON THAT SCALE.

QUITE A SIGHT, EH?

DO YOU REALIZE TRUMP COULD HAVE BUILT 800 UNITS OF LOW-INCOME HOUSING WITH WHAT HE PAID FOR THAT THING?

LATER...

WELL?

AS YOU SUSPECTED, BIG GUY! THEY LOVE YA!

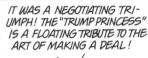 ...AND WHILE EVERYONE ELSE WAS WAITING FOR THE PRICE TO GO DOWN, I STEPPED IN WITH $30 MILLION CASH AND SNAPPED UP A BOAT WHOSE REPLACEMENT VALUE IS $180 MILLION!

IT WAS A NEGOTIATING TRIUMPH! THE "TRUMP PRINCESS" IS A FLOATING TRIBUTE TO THE ART OF MAKING A DEAL!

HEE, HEE!

WHAT'S SO FUNNY, CAPTAIN?

NOTHING'S FUNNY, SIR. I JUST LOVE THAT YOU CALL DEAL-MAKING AN "ART."

CLASSY, HUH? IT WAS MY WIFE'S IDEA.

IT REALLY PUTS PAINTING AND LITERATURE IN THEIR PLACE.

I GUESS COMING DOWN HERE WAS A GOOD IDEA, MR. TRUMP! LOOK AT THE RECEPTION YOU'RE GETTING!

WELL, OF COURSE, CAPTAIN! WHETHER IN ATLANTIC CITY OR NEW ORLEANS, THERE WILL ALWAYS BE AN AUDIENCE FOR QUALITY!

THESE ARE MY PEOPLE, CAPTAIN, THE STRIVERS, THE WANNA-BES, THE LITTLE PEOPLE WITH BIG DREAMS!

YOO-HOO! DONALD! OVER HERE!

WARNING!

YOU SEEN THE VICE PRESIDENT, SENATOR?

NO, HE DIDN'T MAKE IT. FROM WHAT I HEAR, HIS HANDLERS ARE KEEPING HIM UNDER WRAPS UNTIL TOMORROW.

THEY FIGURE REAGAN'S RECEPTION IN THE BOWL TONIGHT COULD PROVE EMBARRASSING.

EMBARRASSING? THAT'S PUTTING IT MILDLY.

FOUR MORE YEARS! FOUR MORE YEARS!

SIGH...

THANK YOU VERY MUCH, LADIES AND GENTLEMEN. IT'S GOOD TO BE BACK.

THE PEOPLE HERE AT TRUMP PLAZA TOLD ME Y'ALL WANTED TO HEAR MY OLD HITS, SONGS LIKE "HEARTBREAK HOTEL" AND "DON'T BE CRUEL..."

BUT I TOLD 'EM, I GOTTA BE ME. TONIGHT I WANNA PLAY SOMETHIN' DIFFERENT FOR Y'ALL. LADIES AND GENTLEMEN, THE MUSIC OF MY GOOD FRIEND, MR. JOHN DENVER!

DAMN... DID YOU CALL THE RIOT POLICE?

THEY'RE ON ALERT.

ROCKY MOUNTAIN HIIIGH!

IT'S AN OUTRAGE! FIRST THE GUY CHARGED $1500 A TICKET FOR A 90-SECOND FIGHT! NOW HE'S RIPPED OFF $2500 A HEAD TO SEE SOME BLIMPO ELVIS IMPOSTER SING "ROCKY MOUNTAIN HIGH"!

I'M ROLAND HEDLEY. IT'S A BAD NIGHT FOR CASINO OPERATOR DON TRUMP AS HIS MUCH BALLY-HOOED RETURN OF ELVIS HAS ERUPTED INTO UGLY MAYHEM.

ANOTHER CLEAR LOSER HERE TONIGHT: GEORGE BUSH, WHOSE CAMPAIGN APPEARANCE HAS BEEN COMPLETELY UPSTAGED BY THE VIOLENT REACTION TO THE ABORTED CONCERT.

...AND IF I'M ELECTED, I DARN SURE WON'T BURN THE FLAG!

KILL TRUMP! KILL TRUMP!

THE BOSS SUMMONS DUKE FOR THEIR WEEKLY CONFAB.

...AND MY WIFE WILL BOARD TODAY. SEND A LITTER.

CHECK.

OH, ONE MORE THING. I'VE HIRED A NEW SOCIAL DI-RECTOR.

SOCIAL DIRECTOR?

YEAH. I'D LIKE YOU TO MEET HER. MARILYN, SEND IN MISS HUAN.

HOLD IT...

FATE! THERE'S NO OTHER WORD FOR IT, SIR!

CAN YOU BELIEVE IT, SIR? THE WINDS OF DESTINY HAVE TOSSED US TOGETHER AGAIN!

ISN'T IT GREAT, SIR? A FRESH START! A CHANCE TO SHIP OUT AND SHAPE UP TOGETHER! WHO *SAYS* THERE ARE NO SECOND ACTS IN AMERICA? SIR? HELLO?

CAPTAIN, YOU DON'T SEEM TOO THRILLED TO SEE THIS YOUNG WOMAN...

SHE'S JUST A FLASHBACK, SIR. SHE'LL GO AWAY.

NO, SIR, IT'S REALLY ME! TOUCH ME! DISCREETLY, OF COURSE.

SO MUCH HAS HAPPENED SINCE WE SAW EACH OTHER LAST, SIR...

I WAS AFRAID OF THAT.

FIRST, WE HAD A LABOR DISPUTE AT DR. WHOOPEE, AND A DISGRUNTLED FORMER EMPLOYEE ATTACKED ME IN THE EXECUTIVE WASHROOM WITH A SPATULA...

AFTER THAT, I HAD A TORRID PLATONIC RELATIONSHIP WITH A CAPO FROM THE GAMBINO FAMILY, WHICH ENDED WHEN I TOLD HIM I WANTED HIS BABY. THEN I HAD A SELF-DESTRUCTIVE CRUSH ON...

HEY! DID I ASK? DID I ASK?

NO, SIR. AND FRANKLY, I'M A LITTLE HURT.

...AND THEN A FRIEND OF A FRIEND INTRODUCED ME TO MRS. TRUMP'S PERSONNEL DIRECTOR!

SO EVERYTHING TURNED OUT GREAT, ALTHOUGH FOR A WHILE THERE THINGS LOOKED PRETTY GRIM...

IT TOOK ME A LONG TIME TO GET OVER BEING ATTACKED BY THAT MADMAN WITH A SPATULA. THE POLICE NEVER IDENTIFIED HIM.

IT WAS ME.

WELL, I THOUGHT SO, BUT I COULDN'T FIND YOU IN THE MUG BOOK.

DAY 20.

IT'S A MESS DOWN THERE, SIR. WE'RE BASICALLY BUILDING ALL OF PANAMA'S GOVERNING INSTITUTIONS FROM SCRATCH!

WHAT WE URGENTLY NEED IS A CIVILIAN ADMINISTRATOR, SOMEONE ON THE GROUND WHO CAN DIRECT THE RECONSTRUCTION OF THE COUNTRY!

GOT ANYONE IN MIND?

YES, SIR. A RETIRED FOREIGN SERVICE OFFICER WITH GOOD COLONIAL EXPERIENCE. HE'LL DO IT IF WE CAN SETTLE ON A TITLE.

©B Trudeau

OKAY, HOW ABOUT "MAXIMUM PROCONSUL"?

DONE! FAX MY CONTRACT TO SOUTHERN COMMAND!

SORRY, DUKE, I CAN'T SPARE YOU. I'M GONNA HOLD YOU TO YOUR CONTRACT!

BUT MR. T, THIS APPOINTMENT TO PANAMA IS A **MAJOR** OPPORTUNITY...

PANAMA CITY IS THE NEXT HAVANA, THE NEXT SAIGON! IT'S WIDE OPEN, AND AS PROCONSUL, **I'LL** BE MAKING THE DECISIONS ON DEVELOPMENT—HOUSING, HOTELS, CASINOS, THE WORKS!

DON'T BE A STRANGER.

AYE, AYE, SIR!

©B Trudeau

SIR, MAY I BE THE FIRST TO CONGRATULATE YOU ON YOUR APPOINTMENT TO MAXIMUM PROCONSUL OF PANAMA. I ONLY WISH I COULD JOIN YOU!

UNFORTUNATELY, SINCE OUR DIVORCE, I'VE DEVELOPED ROOTS AND COMMITMENTS RIGHT HERE IN NEW JERSEY. I HAVE A NICE HOME THAT I'VE JUST DECORATED...

...AND I HAVE TWO CATS AND FOUR PLANTS THAT NEED ME. I ALSO HAVE A JOB I LOVE, FOR WHICH I AM BOTH APPRECIATED AND WELL-COMPENSATED!

WHAT A SHAME. I NEED SOMEONE TO TASTE MY FOOD.

I'LL GO PACK.

©B Trudeau

DAY 24. PROCONSUL DUKE MEETS THE PRESS ON A SWELTERING HOWARD AIR FORCE BASE TARMAC.

I'M ONLY GOING TO SAY THIS ONCE...

MY MISSION HERE IS TO REBUILD A BASICALLY DYSFUNCTIONAL NATION, A COUNTRY WITH NO POLICE FORCE, NO CALL-WAITING, AND NOT A SINGLE DECENT MEXICAN RESTAURANT!

I DON'T WANT TO PUT ANY TIMETABLES ON THIS, BUT MY GUESS IS WE'LL BE OUT OF HERE WELL BEFORE THE '92 NEW HAMPSHIRE PRIMARY. ANY QUESTIONS?

YES, YOU WITH THE TENTACLES AND MELTING EYEBALLS.

MR. DUKE, HAVE YOU LICKED YOUR DRUG PROBLEM YET?

MAN, LOOK AT THE NEIGHBORHOOD NEAR THE COMANDANCIA!

THEY SAY HUNDREDS OF CIVILIANS LOST THEIR LIVES, SIR.

YEAH, WELL, BUSH SAID THE BODY COUNT WAS WORTH IT, SO THAT'S GOOD ENOUGH FOR ME!

YES, SIR.

LOOK, HONEY! IF PEOPLE LIKE YOU HADN'T CALLED HIM A WIMP, WE WOULDN'T EVEN BE HERE!

I KNOW, SIR. WE ALL BEAR RESPONSIBILITY.

SO HOW'S THE NEW PROCONSUL WORKING OUT?

MIXED REPORTS, SIR.

AT LAST WEEKEND'S EMBASSY RECEPTION, HE SPILLED A PITCHER OF DAIQUIRIS ON VICE PRESIDENT CALDERON AND LATER FELL INTO THE POOL...

ON THE OTHER HAND, HE'S GOTTEN PERSONALLY INVOLVED IN RESTORING CIVIL PEACE. HE'S EVEN BEEN TEACHING CLASSES AT THE NEW "PUBLIC FORCE" ACADEMY!

GOOD MORNING. THIS IS AN ELECTRIC CATTLE PROD.

PSST! SIR! THAT'S BEEN DROPPED FROM THE SYLLABUS!

PROCONSUL DUKE TALKS TO PANAMA'S NEW "PUBLIC FORCE."

THE IMPORTANT THING FOR YOU TO REMEMBER IS THAT IN THE NEW PANAMA, YOU GOTTA GO BY THE BOOK— OUR BOOK!

NOW, I DON'T LIKE IT ANY MORE THAN YOU, BUT THAT'S THE DOWN SIDE OF A REAL DEMOCRACY— FOR SOME REASON, CRIMINALS HAVE RIGHTS!

WHAT KIND OF RIGHTS, SEÑOR PRO-CONSUL?

UM...WELL, FOR STARTERS, YOU CAN'T DO ANY-THING CRUEL OR UNU-SUAL.

BUT YOUR SOLDIERS MADE NORI-EGA LISTEN TO RAP MUSIC FOR A WEEK!

THAT WAS STILL PART OF THE INVASION. DOESN'T COUNT.

SEÑOR, WILL WE GET TO WEAR ITALIAN SPORTS JACKETS?

MEN, AS PANAMA'S NEW PEACE OFFICERS, IT'LL BE UP TO YOU TO MAKE THIS A COUNTRY WE CAN ALL BE PROUD OF!

PANAMA'S BEING GIVEN ONE MORE CHANCE TO EMULATE THE AMERI-CAN MODEL OF DEMOCRACY. YOU HAVE A FREELY ELECTED PRESI-DENT, YOU HAVE A CONSTITU-TION, YOU HAVE FOUNDING FATHERS...

WHAT FOUNDING FATHERS?

THE 82ND AIRBORNE. REVERE THEM.

HOW ABOUT A DECLARA-TION OF INDEPEN-DENCE?

DON'T GET CUTE. CLASS DISMISSED.

LISTEN, COLONEL, AFTER WE CLEAR OUT OF HERE, YOU CAN GO BACK TO YOUR OWN WAY OF KEEPING ORDER! BUT UNTIL THEN, I'VE GOT A DEMOCRACY TO RUN!

YOU'VE GOT TO FIND A FEW MEN FOR THE PUBLIC FORCE WHO WEREN'T IN THE P.D.F.! EVERYONE THINKS ALL WE'VE DONE IS CHANGE THE SHOULDER PATCHES!

SI, SEÑOR PROCONSUL, BUT THE PEOPLE RESPECT MY MEN!

ARE YOU KIDDING? THEY LOATHE THEM! 92% OF THE PANAMANIAN PEO-PLE SUPPORT THE INVASION!

IF YOU SAY SO, SEÑOR. SHOULD WE DETAIN THE OTHER 8%?

YOU STILL DON'T GET IT, DO YOU?

THE PROCONSUL GETS A CALL.

MR. DUKE? THIS IS THE PRESIDENT! HOW'S DANNY MAKING OUT?

WELL, HE'S MAKIN'A HELLUVA IMPRESSION, SIR!

I WAS AFRAID OF THAT. WHAT'S HE DOING NOW?

INSPECTING THE INVASION FORCE, SIR. HE'S WORRIED ABOUT THEIR UNIFORMS.

THEIR UNIFORMS? WHAT'S WRONG WITH THEM?

THEY'RE JUNGLE-STYLE CAMOUFLAGE, SIR. THE VICE PRESIDENT THINKS THEY'RE INAPPROPRIATE FOR URBAN COMBAT.

CAN WE GET UNIFORMS WITH LITTLE BUILDINGS ON THEM?

WE'LL TRY, SIR!

SO HOW ARE THE TROOPS, MR. VICE PRESIDENT?

GOOD! THEY LOOKED TAN, RESTED, NOT AT ALL LIKE THEY'D BEEN IN AN INVASION!

THE ONLY PROBLEM IS THEY'RE STILL HERE. THE WHOLE REASON I CAME DOWN HERE WAS TO REASSURE OUR FRIENDS THAT THIS WAS A SHORT-TERM, ONE-TIME INTERVENTION!

IT'S NOT EASY CARRYING A MESSAGE LIKE THAT ALL OVER LATIN AMERICA—TO COUNTRIES LIKE...LIKE...WHAT'S THAT ONE WITH THE BEACHES?

WHATEVER.

RIGHT. ESPECIALLY IF YOU DON'T SPEAK A **WORD** OF LATIN!

PRESIDENT VARGAS? PROCONSUL DUKE HERE! LISTEN, I GOT DAN QUAYLE HERE SITTING IN MY OFFICE...

HE'S MADE A HECK OF AN EFFORT TO GET DOWN HERE. AND I THINK MORE OF YOU GUYS SHOULD BE HEARING HIM OUT...

WHAT IF HE FLEW DOWN TO BOGOTA—UNOFFICIALLY, OF COURSE—AND EXPLAINED OUR POSITION?...RIGHT... RIGHT... UH-HUH...I SEE...

HE'S AFRAID YOU'LL BE DRAGGED FROM YOUR LIMO AND BEATEN WITH PIPES.

DAMN... OKAY, LET'S TRY THE PRESIDENT OF PUERTO RICO!

LOOK, PRESIDENT ARIAS, I APPRECIATE YOUR POSITION, BUT COME ON, THE INVASION WASN'T DANNY QUAYLE'S CALL! **NOTHING** IS! WHY TAKE IT OUT ON HIM?

BECAUSE THE NATIONS OF THIS REGION HAVE HAD ENOUGH, MR. PROCONSUL.

ENOUGH? ENOUGH OF WHAT?

IN 1901, THE U.S. SENT TROOPS TO COLOMBIA; IN 1902, TO PANAMA; IN 1903, HONDURAS, DOMINICAN REPUBLIC AND PANAMA; IN 1904, DOMINICAN REPUBLIC AND PANAMA; 1906, CUBA; 1907, HONDURAS; 1910, NICARAGUA; 1911, HONDURAS; 1912...

WELL? WELL?

BAD LUCK. HE'S A HISTORY NUT.

LOOK, PRESIDENT GARCIA PEREZ, YOU'VE GOT TO TAKE THE LONG VIEW HERE! SOONER OR LATER, BUSH IS GONNA SEND QUAYLE TO PERU WHETHER YOU LIKE IT OR NOT!

WHY NOT JUST GET IT OVER WITH? WHAT?...UH-HUH...RIGHT... HOW WOULD THAT WORK? UH-HUH... OKAY, LET ME FLY IT BY HIM.

HE SAYS YOU CAN COME IF YOU SLIP ACROSS THE BOLIVIAN BORDER, DON A DISGUISE AND RIDE BY BURRO 250 MILES TO A REMOTE MONASTERY OUTSIDE OF CUZCO, WHERE YOU WOULD MEET WITH A RANKING GOVERNMENT OFFICIAL.

A **RANKING** OFFICIAL? WOW...

ALERT THE MONKS.

WERE YOU ABLE TO OPEN ANY DOORS FOR THE VEEP, SIR?

YEAH, POSSIBLY PERU.

GARCIA PEREZ SAYS HE CAN COME AS LONG AS HE'S WILLING TO PUT ON A DISGUISE AND RIDE A DONKEY THROUGH THE ANDES FOR A SECRET MEET AT A MONASTERY.

DANNY'S GAME, BUT HE'S STILL GOTTA RUN IT BY THE BIG GUY.

DANNY, COME HOME.

AW, SIR! I ALREADY GOT MY DISGUISE!

DID MR. QUAYLE EVER MAKE IT TO PERU, SIR?

NOPE...

HE GOT CALLED BACK TO WASHINGTON AT THE LAST MINUTE.

MY GUESS IS THEY WANT HIM IN PLACE IN CASE THE CHIEF GETS WAXED ON HIS WAY DOWN TO THE DRUG CONFERENCE.

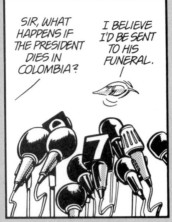

SIR, WHAT HAPPENS IF THE PRESIDENT DIES IN COLOMBIA?

I BELIEVE I'D BE SENT TO HIS FUNERAL.

IN PANAMA, THE BLOOM IS OFF THE INVASION...

WHAT DID BUSH BRING US BUT **MORE** POVERTY AND DEATH?

THOUSANDS OF OUR HOMES WERE DESTROYED, BUT **STILL** WE SEE NO AID! WE MUST TAKE OUR COUNTRY **BACK**! WE MUST SEND THE PROCONSUL **PACKING**!

YANQUI GO HOME! YANQUI GO HOME!

NOT MUCH OF A LIKENESS.

CLOSE ENOUGH, SIR.

ANTI–U.S. **RIOTS**! AFTER ALL I'VE DONE FOR THIS RAT-HOLE OF A COUNTRY!

I CAN IMAGINE HOW THAT MIGHT BE DEMORAL-IZING, SIR...

BUT LOOK AT IT FROM THE PANAMAN-IAN PERSPECTIVE. JUST TO ARREST A DRUG DEALER, U.S. FORCES MANAGED TO INFLICT $2 BILLION WORTH OF DAMAGE ON THE COUNTRY.

IN THE ABSENCE OF NO AID WHATSOEVER, THOUSANDS ARE STILL HOMELESS. SOME ARE EVEN LIVING UNDER CLUS-TERS OF PARACHUTES ABANDONED BY THE VERY SOLDIERS WHOSE ARRIVAL LEFT THEM HOMELESS!

CHEAP, THIRD WORLD **IRONY**! I WON'T **STAND** FOR IT!

THEY CALL IT "SCREAMING EAGLE ESTATES."

ZIP!

I DON'T BELIEVE IT! YOU WERE RIGHT, HONEY! THERE *ARE* PEOPLE LIVING UNDER PARACHUTES!

YES, SIR. FOR FOUR MONTHS NOW.

THIS IS INCREDIBLE! LIKE SOME NIGHTMARISH POST-MODERN WHITE SALE.

ACTUALLY, SIR, IT'S INVASION LITTER...

...BUT WITHOUT IT, THESE PEOPLE WOULD HAVE NO SHELTER AT ALL! IT MEANS A LOT YOUR COMING DOWN HERE, SIR. IT SHOWS YOU *CARE*!

YEAH, BUT I DON'T. THIS WOULD MAKE A HELLUVA THEME PARK, WOULDN'T IT?

YOU CAN'T FOOL ME, SIR.

SEÑORA! I'M TOLD YOU AND OTHERS MAKE YOUR *HOMES* HERE AMONG THE PARACHUTES! HOW REMARKABLE!

THERE'S SOMETHING *VISIONARY* HERE! PARACHUTE DOMICILES! COOL, DRY, STRONG, ILLUMINATED BY SOFT, FILTERED LIGHT! THIS IS THE FUTURE! IT WORKS!

I SEE A CITY, *SEÑORA*! A *SILK* CITY! 1,000 SHIMMERING UNITS STRUNG ACROSS THE HILLS! WHAT DO YOU SAY TO *THAT*?

LAST NIGHT, WE BURNED YOU IN EFFIGY.

OKAY, *2,000*! BUT ANY MORE AND YOU'LL ATTRACT RODENTS.

CITIZENS OF PANAMA! WHAT YOU HAVE BUILT HERE IS NOTHING SHORT OF FANTASTIC! FROM THESE DISCARDED SHROUDS YOU HAVE FASHIONED YOUR OWN SALVATION!

IT IS NOW MY PRIVILEGE TO DEDICATE "SCREAMING EAGLE ESTATES" TO THE MEMORY OF YOUR FOUNDING FATHERS — THE 82ND AIRBORNE! *CHEERS*!

C'MON, HONEY, LET'S GET TO OUR NEXT APPOINTMENT! BY *GOD*, I'M GLAD I SAW THIS WITH MY OWN EYES!

SIR, WHAT'D WE HAVE FOR BREAKFAST?

NOTHING SPECIAL. ONE DAY, THIS WILL *ALL* BE YOURS, HONEY!

219

Panel 1: GOOD EVENING, FOLKS! I'D LIKE TO WELCOME YOU TO CLUB SCUD, ESPECIALLY THE OIL WELL CAPPERS FROM RED ADAIR AND THE OTHER TEXAN OUTFITS!

Panel 2: I THINK YOU'LL FIND OUR ESTABLISHMENT AN OASIS OF GOOD CHEER AND REFRESHMENT IN THE OTHERWISE DRY AND BLASTED LANDSCAPE THAT IS POST-WAR KUWAIT!

Panel 3: WHETHER IT'S THE IMPECCABLY MIXED COCKTAILS OR THE CRISPLY STARCHED TABLECLOTHS, WE HAVE SPARED NO EFFORT IN MAKING YOUR CLUB A PLACE OF DISTINCTION AND CLASS!

Panel 4: NOW THEN, SOMEONE ASKED ME ABOUT OUR MISS DESERT STORM WET T-SHIRT CONTEST...

THAT WAS ME. I WAS JUST CURIOUS.

Panel 5: SORRY THE BOYS AIN'T SCRUBBED TODAY. OUR WATER LINE WENT DOWN...

FINE WITH ME, SIR. I **LIKE** THE MANLY SCENT OF SWEET CRUDE!

Panel 6: WELL, YOU KINDA **HAVE** TO IF YOU'RE GONNA HANG WITH WELL-KILLERS! WE DO GET DOUSED WITH JUICE! SOMETIMES OUR OWN **WIVES** CAN'T TELL US APART. HEE, HEE!

Panel 7: HEE...

Panel 8: PROBABLY WHY I'M ON MY FIFTH MARRIAGE.

I WAS GOING TO SAY.

Panel 9: MAN...WHAT A DAY! RAN OVER **ANOTHER** LAWN DART!

WHAT'S A LAWN DART, SIR? SOUNDS DANGEROUS.

Panel 10: UNEXPLODED CLUSTER BOMB. BLEW A TREAD CLEAN OFF MY BULLDOZER!

WOW...YOU KNOW, **YOU** GUYS ARE THE HEROES NOW!

Panel 11: UH-HUH... HEY, LISTEN, KID, YOU WANT A FRIENDLY PIECE OF ADVICE?

FROM YOU, SIR? I'D BE HONORED!

Panel 12: GET A HAIRCUT. YOU LOOK LIKE A GIRL.

THANK YOU, SIR.

KUWAIT HIGH SCHOOL 1991 YEARBOOK

*W*hat a year it's been for the seniors! First, classes were suspended for the fall and winter. Most of us left for Cairo or Gstaad. Then, liberation! What a hoot! As Prince Tariq "Disco" Al-Amiri put it, "Saddam Hussein can eat my shorts!" Even with no classes, five guys got into Princeton and three into UCLA, so the year wasn't a total loss. Also, there was the senior prom -- talk about a blast! Thanks to Sheik al-Sabah for letting us use his townhouse in London, and to the whole class for showing so much spirit. Go, Scorpions!

YOUSSEF AL-MIAZ
"Al" "The Man"
Class President... Slept through the invasion... Treasurer for neighborhood resistance cell... "Grow up!"...Quote: "Down with the dens of treason and shame, as mentioned in our previous communique."

HAMED AL-MESBAH
"Ham" "Pee-Wee"
Vice President... illegal editorial... weenie reforms ... boycotted Emir's party... working at McDonald's... "sweet spot" on a baseball... Ambition: "to move Kuwait into the 15th century."

ABDEL AL-SABAH
"Prince" "Your Majesty"
Class Treasurer... "I'm outa here!"... Christmas in Aspen... Waterbombing his bodyguard... CNN freak... Bootsie in Bahrain... Trying to grow a mustache...Gold sneaker eyelets... Polo I, II.

AHMAD SALMAN
"Stinky" "Traitor"
Class Secretary... P.L.O. donation boxes... Only guy in school who could fix the air conditioning... "Go, Intifada!"... Soccer I, II... Uncle Hussein... Missing for two months.